OTHER ANNOTATED BOOKS BY MARTIN GARDNER

The Annotated Casey at the Bat
The Annotated Alice
More Annotated Alice
The Annotated Ancient Mariner
The Annotated Snark
The Annotated Innocence of Father Brown

SUMMIT BOOKS
New York · London · Toronto · Sydney · Tokyo · Singapore

THE ANNOTATED

Night

Before Christmas

A collection of sequels,
parodies, and imitations
of Clement Moore's
immortal ballad about Santa Claus

Edited, with an introduction and notes, by
MARTIN GARDNER

SUMMIT BOOKS
Simon & Schuster Building
Rockefeller Center
1230 Avenue of the Americas
New York, New York 10020

10 9 8 7 6 5 4 3 2 1

Library of Congress Cataloging in Publication Data
The Annotated Night before Christmas : a collection of sequels,
    parodies, and imitations of Clement Moore's immortal ballad about
    Santa Claus / edited, with an introduction and notes, by Martin
    Gardner.
        p. cm.
    1. Moore, Clement Clarke, 1779–1863—Parodies, imitations, etc.
2. Moore, Clement Clarke, 1779–1863. Night before Christmas.
3. Santa Claus—Poetry. 4. Christmas—Poetry. 5. American poetry.
I. Gardner, Martin, 1914– . II. Moore, Clement Clarke,
1779–1863. Night before Christmas.
PS2429.M5Z54   1991
811'.2—dc20   91-2991
                                                                  CIP

ISBN 0-671-70839-2

To my grandchildren,
Martin and William

CONTENTS

ACKNOWLEDGMENTS

Searching for parodies, sequels, and imitations of Clement Moore's ballad was no easy task. I have many people to thank for assisting me, but especially the following:

Betsy Shirley, who copied items in her great collection of material relating to Santa Claus and Moore, and collectors Carolyn Fox and William Dunning, who were similarly generous.

Mary Catherine E. Johnsen, special collections librarian of the Hunt Library at Carnegie Mellon University, where she allowed me access to the collection of Anne Lyon Haight; Libby Chenault, a reference librarian at the Wilson Library, University of North Carolina, Chapel Hill, who helped me find my way through the Porter Kellam collection; and Carolyn Taylor, special collections librarian of Florida State University, Tallahassee, who allowed me to search its Childhood in Poetry collection.

I also wish to thank Janet Jurist and Russell Barnhart for bibliographic research at the New York Public Library; Michael Patrick Hearn, author of *The Annotated Wizard of Oz*, for valuable leads; Dana Richards, whose request for parodies on his computer bulletin board at the University of Virginia, Charlottesville, yielded so many surprising results; John Mitchell for help on Spanish dialect versions of Moore's poem; Anne Freedgood, my editor at Summit who accepted the project and greatly improved the manuscript; and Donald Olson and Florence Falkow for their scrupulous copy editing.

Special thanks are due to Margery Peters of the Library of The General Society of Mechanics and Tradesmen for her generous assistance in uncovering illustrative material.

INTRODUCTION

"I'm called Mr. Santa Claus"

I hope no one imagines that I regard the selections in this book as good poetry. Although doggerel and great poetry are at opposite ends of various continua, with all shades in between, there is a useful rough distinction between good poetry and what can be called popular verse. Popular verse has an obvious metrical beat and almost always a pattern of rhyme. The meanings of its lines are as clear on a first reading as on a second. Enjoyment may be repeated on each rereading, but it seldom intensifies. Great poetry has both a subtler musicality and less obvious meanings that are seldom grasped completely when the poem is first read.

All of which is simply repeating the distinctions put forth by T. S. Eliot in the introduction to his collection of poems by Rudyard Kipling. As Eliot recognized, Kipling is a splendid example of a writer on the borderline between a great poet and a composer of popular verse. "The Road to Mandalay,'' for instance, almost rises to great poetry even though its music and meanings can be appreciated almost completely on a first reading. And, of course, no English poem has been more effectively set to music.

Popular verse, like good poetry, can vary in aesthetic value, and there is always room for argument about its merits. Let me say without hesitation that I consider most of the parodies in this book doggerel, or close to doggerel, whereas Moore's original ballad, which started it all, is an example of popular verse at its best. I like to think of such verse as similar to popular music. Nobody imagines that a composer of catchy melodies is on the same level as Mozart, yet popular tunes can be good or bad. Sometimes a poem and a tune merge to create a great popular song such as ''The Battle Hymn of the Republic.''

I confess unashamedly that I enjoy popular verse when it is artfully constructed, just as I enjoy hearing good popular melodies. Please do not suppose that I confuse such verse with great poetry. My tastes in poetry run toward the classical; most contemporary poets have reputations that I consider to be vastly inflated. Although I will not be here to verify it, I firmly believe that a hundred years from now Moore's poem, like ''Casey at the Bat'' or ''The Shooting of Dan McGrew,'' will be memorized and recited and enjoyed, whereas no one outside university cloisters will recall a single poem by William Carlos Williams.

The poems that here follow Moore's original are intended for your entertainment and as testimony to the astonishing popularity and influence of Moore's ballad. Please do not take any of them, or their mock-scholarly annotations, too seriously.

The Pudding cometh

Albert E. Sterner.

ONE

Clement
Clarke
Moore

SANTA CLAUS, CLEMENT MOORE, AND CHRISTMAS

"Now, don't laugh too loud. We have come through so many cynical years it gives me a chuckle to think what would happen to anyone in a New York night club who got up and recited my choice heart throb. . . . There are clinging to those illy-written lines a something that brings a real nostalgia of childjoy such as we will never know again. It is not maudlin; it is real. Am I wrong?"

—The artist James Montgomery Flagg, quoted in Favorite Heart Throbs of Famous People *(Grosset and Dunlap, 1929), as he explains to Joe Mitchell Chapple, the book's editor, why he chose "The Night Before Christmas."*

The story of how Clement Clarke Moore came to write his immortal poem, and the curious history of its early anonymous publications, have been told many times. Indeed, every Christmas they seem to be told again in some newspaper or periodical. No one, however, has told it better or in more detail than Burton Egbert Stevenson, an American novelist and anthologist, in his book *Famous Single Poems*.

Stevenson was fascinated by a common literary phe-
nomenon that seems to interest nobody these days except
me. "One swallow may not make a summer," he writes at
the beginning of his introductory chapter, "but one poem
makes a poet. Immortality may be—and often has been—
won with a single song." Stevenson's term for rhymesters
who achieve this is "one-poem men." In many cases such
poets do their best to write "serious" poems in classical style,
poems that can be skillfully crafted and are often gathered
in books. All these strenuous efforts fade into oblivion while
the single poem, to the author's amazement, strikes some
sort of responsive chord in millions of readers that causes it
to outlast by far everything else he or she wrote.

"It is not altogether astonishing that a masterpiece
should live," writes Stevenson, "but, by some curious quirk,
a mere jingle, which possesses no possible claim to inspi-
ration, often proves more immortal than an epic. 'Bo-Peep'
outlives 'Paradise Regained,' and grave and scholarly men,
after a lifetime of labor in their chosen fields, have been
astonished and chagrined to find that their sole claim to
public remembrance rested upon a bit of careless rhyme writ-
ten in a moment of relaxation." Stevenson continues:

Poets have always been the special sport of Fortune, which delights
to play with them, to whirl them aloft and to cast them down, to
torment them with fleeting glimpses of happiness in the midst of
long nightmares of despair, and especially to condemn their fa-
vorite children to swift oblivion and to raise up some despised and
rejected outcast for the admiration of mankind. Nobody—poets
least of all!—has yet discovered the formula which will assure
immortality to a poem. Mere size will not do it—the most ambitious
edifices are usually the first to crumble. Neither polished diction
nor lofty thought will do it—most deathless songs are written in
words of one syllable on the simplest of themes.

Another mark of a poem's popularity, one not men-
tioned by Stevenson, is that other versifiers are moved to
produce sequels and imitations. In my *Annotated Casey at the
Bat* I gathered as many such ballads as I could find about
Mighty Casey, the hero of Mudville, who has become almost
as permanent a fixture in American folklore as Santa Claus.

Ernest L. Thayer, the author of *Casey*, had many other humorous poems published in the *San Francisco Examiner* and other Hearst newspapers, but only *Casey* survived. Stevenson devotes a chapter to this greatest of all baseball poems, and I relied heavily on it in the introduction to my *Casey* anthology, as I will rely here on his chapter about Moore's poem.

"The Night Before Christmas," as Moore's poem has come to be known, has far exceeded even Thayer's ballad in popularity and in the number of its sequels and parodies. No other poem by an American has been printed more often in newspapers, periodicals, and books, or has been illustrated by more graphic artists. The illustrations run the gamut from such sophisticated artists as Arthur Rackham to the primitive simplicity of Grandma Moses, who did her paintings for the poem when she was one hundred years old. I do not know how many times the poem has been set to music, but I know of at least three examples. Sheet music for the ballad, composed by Hanna Van Vollenhoven, was published by the Boston Music Company in 1923. Sheet music for a Decca recording by Fred Waring, the tune composed by Ken Darby and arranged by Harry Simeone, was published in 1945 by Shawnee Press, Delaware Water Gap, Pennsylvania. By far the most successful musical adaption was by the composer Johnny Marks (whom we will meet again in our last chapter on Rudolph the Red-Nosed Reindeer). The Saint Nicholas Music Company of New York City published the sheet music in 1952. Rosemary Clooney and Gene Autry recorded the song, as did Mitch Miller, the Ames Brothers, Gisele MacKenzie, and many others.

It is often claimed that Moore's poem has been translated into all the major languages. However, Anne Lyon Haight, in her preface to a catalog for an exhibition of her marvelous collection of early printings of Moore's ballad, has this to say:

I know of no collection, large or small, of editions in other than English. I have advertised for foreign language copies, but with no success. I have written to scores of dealers across this land in an effort to obtain such editions. None was forthcoming. In my travels in Europe, and in other lands, I have sought fruitlessly for these elusive ghosts. The answer is always the same, even in Britain—no one has heard of the poem, nor of Clement C. Moore, and much less of any translation of it. I can only conclude that the reports of the existence of such translations—with one or two exceptions—are nothing less than myths, to be accounted as fabrics of fiction, as ghosts in our records of literature.

The two exceptions mentioned by Mrs. Haight are *Besuch vom Sankt Nikolaus*, a German translation that appeared in the December 21, 1949, issue of *Heute*, a magazine published by the Office of the U.S. High Commissioner for Germany; and *Nuit de Noël*, printed in Paris the same year as one of Simon and Schuster's French series of Little Golden Books, with illustrations by Corinne Malvern. I am told that a later French translation, *La Veilee de Noël*, was published by Grosset and Dunlap in 1962, with pictures by a Japanese artist, Gyo Fujikawa.

Vincent Starrett, a Chicago writer, critic, and poet, was one of the first to amass a collection of book printings of Moore's poem. Many similar collections have been and are being made. Unfortunately, collectors of the poem are seldom interested in acquiring its imitations, and the task of running them down for this curious anthology has not been easy. There is no good way to search for them except in special collections. I have had to rely mostly on verse I happened to stumble upon and poems remembered by friends. I am under no illusion about the number of gems I have probably missed. Hundreds, perhaps thousands, of parodies have no doubt been printed in newspapers, periodicals, and on Christmas cards, since Moore's poem was first published.

Clement Clarke Moore was the only child of the Right Reverend Benjamin Moore, a bishop of the Protestant Episcopal Church in New York City and rector of Trinity Church on Wall Street. He was also president of Columbia College, now Columbia University. During the Revolution he never wavered in his loyalty to England. When Alexander Hamilton lay dying after his duel with Aaron Burr, it was Benjamin Moore who gave him the last rites. Benjamin's wife, Charity, inherited a large tract of farm and orchard land between Nineteenth and Twenty-fourth streets, extending from Eighth Avenue to the Hudson River, on Manhattan's West Side. It was in the family mansion on this property, within what is now called the Chelsea section of Manhattan, that Clement was born in 1779.

Moore received a bachelor of arts degree from Columbia in 1798. He had intended to become a minister but changed his mind, and devoted himself instead to classical and Oriental studies. His *Compendious Lexicon of the Hebrew Language*, two volumes published in 1809, was the first English-Hebrew lexicon printed in the United States. When the General Theological Seminary of the Episcopal Church was organized, he gave it the land between Ninth and Tenth avenues and between Twentieth and Twenty-first streets. Here the seminary buildings were built and still stand. Three years later he became a professor of Greek and Oriental literature at the seminary. After his death in 1863 he was buried in the Trinity Church cemetery at 155th Street and Amsterdam Avenue.

Every year, in late December, a Clement Clarke Moore Christmas Commemoration is held in the Church of the Intercession at Broadway and 155th Street in uptown Manhattan. After the candlelight service, at which Moore's ballad is read, there is a lantern procession, with luck through snow, to Moore's grave across the street. The 1991 Commemoration will be the eightieth.

It was in the winter of 1822 that Moore, in a light-hearted mood, dashed off his famous ballad to read at Christmas to

The Theological Seminary of the Protestant Episcopal Church, Ninth Avenue and 20–21 Streets, New York City in 1841

THE NEW-YORK HISTORICAL SOCIETY

his two daughters, seven-year-old Margaret and six-year-old Charity. (A third daughter, three-year-old Mary, was too young to appreciate the poem.) Present during the reading was either Harriet Butler, daughter of David Butler, then rector of St. Paul's Episcopal Church in Troy, New York, or a friend of hers. In either case, Harriet copied the poem in her "album," a book that young ladies of the time liked to keep, so that she could read it to the children at her husband's rectory.

Just before Christmas, a year later, an unknown woman (most likely Mrs. Butler) gave a copy of Moore's poem to the editor of the Troy *Sentinel*, without telling him who wrote it. The poem was published on the second page of the Tuesday, December 23, 1823, issue with the title "Account of a Visit from St. Nicholas." It was preceded by the following note by Orville Luther Holley, the paper's editor:

We know not to whom we are indebted for the following description of that unwearied patron of children—that homely, but delightful personification of parental kindness—Sante Claus, his costume and his equipage, as he goes about visiting the fire-sides of this happy land, laden with Christian bounties; but, from whomever it may have come, we give thanks for it. There is, to our apprehension, a spirit of cordial goodness in it, a playfulness of fancy, and a benevolent alacrity to enter into the feelings and promote the simple pleasures of children, which are altogether charming. We hope our little patrons, both lads and lassies, will accept it as proof of our unfeigned good will toward them—as a token of our warmest wish that they may have many a merry Christmas; that they may long retain their beautiful relish for those unbought, homebred joys, which derive their flavor from filial piety and fraternal love, and which they may be assured are the least alloyed that time can furnish them; and that they may never depart from that simplicity of character, which is their own fairest ornament, and for the sake of which they have been pronounced, by authority which none can gainsay, the types of such as shall inherit the kingdom of heaven.

The fifty-six-line poem was such an instant success with readers that for several years the *Sentinel* reprinted it each Christmas and about 1830 began issuing it as a broadside, with a woodcut by Myron King showing Santa sailing over rooftops in his sleigh. The sheet was handed out by carriers when they delivered the paper's Christmas edition.

Not until seven years later was the question raised about the poem's origin. Who was the author, the New York *Courier* wanted to know, when it printed the ballad on January 1, 1829. On January 20, Holley answered the query:

A few days since, the editors of the New York *Courier*, at the request of a lady, inserted some lines descriptive of one of the visits of that good old Dutch Saint, St. Nicholas, and at the same time applied to our Albany neighbors for information as to the author. That information, we apprehend, the Albany editors cannot give. The lines were *first* published in this paper. They came to us from a manuscript in possession of a lady of this city. We have been given to understand that the author of them belongs, by birth and residence, to the city of New York, and that he is a gentleman of *more* merit as a scholar and a writer than many more of more noisy pretensions.

Holley's italicizing of *more* in his last sentence, and his use of it two more times, suggests that he knew who the author was, but respected Moore's desire not to have his name associated with what he considered insignificant doggerel. At any rate, the many reprintings of the poem over the next eight years, in all parts of the country, carried no byline. In 1837 *The New York Book of Poetry*, published by George Dearborn, contained the ballad and for the first time identified Moore as the author. Seven years later Moore included the poem in his own collection, a book titled simply *Poems*, published in New York by Bartlett and Welford. Most of the poems in this book are deadly serious. Here is how Stevenson describes them:

He invokes the Muses, celebrates various nymphs, apostrophizes Hebe, Apollo, Terpsichore, Pallas and numerous other gods and goddesses, and capitalizes Fancy, Hope and so on, all in the good old way. He castigates the follies of the times, especially the freedom with which young ladies display their charms; decries the wine-bibber and exalts the drinker of water; writes at length (fifty pages) of a family excursion to Saratoga; tells of his sorrow at the death of his wife, and includes a few translations from classic poets.

In a word, the volume is entirely characteristic of the times, when writing verses was a sort of courtly accomplishment with which the gravest men were supposed to amuse their leisure hours.

Some of the poems, notably the one about Saint Nicholas, were intended for amusement. In his preface, Moore apologized for them in the following letter to his children:

MY DEAR CHILDREN:

In compliance with your wishes, I here present you with a volume of verses, written by me at different periods of my life.

I have not made a selection from among my verses of such as are of any particular cast; but have given you the melancholy and the lively; the serious, the sportive, and even the trifling; such as relate solely to our own domestic circle, and those of which the subjects take a wider range. Were I to offer you nothing but what is gay and lively, you well know that the deepest and keenest feelings of your father's heart would not be portrayed. If, on the other hand, nothing but what is serious or sad had been presented to your view, an equally imperfect character of his mind would have been exhibited. For you are all aware that he is far from following the school of Chesterfield with regard to harmless mirth and merriment; and that, in spite of all the cares and sorrows of this life, he thinks we are so constituted that a good honest hearty laugh, which conceals no malice, and is excited by nothing corrupt, however ungenteel it may be, is healthful to both body and mind. Another reason why the mere trifles in this volume have not been withheld is that such things have been often found by me to afford greater pleasure than what was by myself esteemed of more worth.

Not until 1848 was the poem published singly in an illustrated edition by the New York firm of Henry M. Onderdonk. Its woodcuts by T. C. Boyd are faithful to Moore's poem in showing reindeer the size of cats, and a Santa small enough to emerge from the huge chimneys and fireplaces of the time. Dodd, Mead reprinted this rare little book in 1971, adding a life of Moore, his wife, and relatives, and included a photograph of the poem as handwritten by Moore in 1862.

In 1897 William S. Pelletreau, in another small book titled *The Visit of St. Nicholas*, told for the first time the full story of how the poem was written and came to be published in the Troy newspaper. No one has questioned the authenticity of this account except the descendants of one Henry Livingston, born in 1748, who lived on an estate in Poughkeepsie, New York. The Livingston family stoutly maintained that their ancestor was the true author of the ballad. Somehow it found its way into Moore's hands, they claimed, and Moore was unable to disown it once it had been attributed to him. Stevenson carefully considers the Livingston claim and roundly rejects it. The sole basis for it seems to be that Livingston did write some verses in anapest meter, but, as Stevenson says, all anapestic verse sounds the same.

One of the most interesting things about Moore's classic is the extent to which it shaped America's greatest myth— almost its only great myth: that of Santa Claus.

True, Santa had his misty antecedents, but they bore little resemblance to him. Saint Nicholas, a fourth-century bishop of Myra (now Kale), a seaport in Asia Minor, was tall, thin, and dignified. Venerated throughout the middle ages, he even became a patron saint in Greece and Russia. His feast day on December 6 was a traditional holiday in Europe until the Reformation, when he fell into disrepute, especially in Protestant countries. Eventually his feast day merged with December 25, which since the fourth century had been Rome's traditional day for celebrating the birth of Jesus. The English word *Christmas* is a compression of the Roman Catholic "Mass of Christ."

Although Holland was Protestant, for some reason Saint Nicholas survived there as a Christmas gift-bringer. For six centuries Dutch children have put their shoes by the fireplace on St. Nicholas Eve (December 5), along with food for the saint's horse. During the night, Sinterklass and his Moorish assistant Zwarte Piet (Black Peter) arrive by ship from, of all places, Spain. The saint gallops through the heavens on his white horse, from roof to roof, with Black Peter somehow following. It is the Moor who pops down chimneys to leave gifts, while Sinterklass, not wanting to soil his white robe and red cassock, drops candy down the chimney and into the waiting shoes.

In other nations, other legendary gift-bearers make annual midwinter visits to homes. There is Father Christmas

in England and France (where he is called Père Noël), though in recent decades Santa Claus and Father Christmas have become interchangeable names in England. Germany's history of Santa Claus counterparts is long and confusing. Shortly after the Reformation, Saint Nicholas was disguised as Christkindel (Christ child), and usually depicted with a halo and riding a white donkey. It is unclear whether this was the child Jesus or a boy or girl sent by Jesus. Accompanying the Christ child was a black-faced ogre known by various names, of which Knecht Ruprecht was apparently the most common.

According to Phillip Snyder's "St. Nicholas and His Counterparts," a chapter in his *December 25: The Joys of Christmas Past*, there were other legendary German gift-bringers, such as Pelznickel (Nicholas in furs)—the Pennsylvania Germans called him Belsnikel or Belsh Nickel—and Weihnachtsmann (Old Father Christmas). Early German settlers in Pennsylvania corrupted Christkindel to Kriss Kringle, apparently the most popular counterpart of Santa in Germany today. Snyder speaks of two early books published in Philadelphia: *Kriss Kringle's Book* (1842), and *Kriss Kringle's Christmas Tree* (1845). Today Kriss Kringle, both here and in Germany, is another name for Santa Claus.

In Italy, the gifts are distributed by the good witch Befana. According to an ancient Christian legend, Befana was sweeping her house when the Three Wise Men rode by and invited her to go with them to Bethlehem. Befana said she was too busy. Later, regretting her decision, she began wandering about the world under a curse that does not allow her to die. Each year on the eve of Twelfth Night (January 5), the day that commemorates the visit of the Magi, Befana slides down the chimney on her broom to fill shoes and stockings with candy and small toys, always peering into the faces of sleeping children, hoping to see the infant Jesus.

In Spain, on the eve of Twelfth Night, it is the Wise Men themselves, arriving by camels on their way to Bethlehem, who bring gifts to children.

In Russia, before the Communists took over, Befana had

Knecht Ruprecht

a counterpart—an old peasant woman called Babushka—and also Saint Nicholas, who would leave presents around a decorated fir tree on January 7 (in the Russian calendar). Communist leaders abolished the holiday. Now it is Grandfather Frost, accompanied by the Snow Maiden, who brings the toys on New Year's Eve. The tree is called a New Year's tree. With fresh winds starting to blow through the Soviet Union, perhaps Saint Nicholas and Babushka will make a comeback. In any case, Grandfather Frost is a fat old fellow in a red suit who looks just like Santa Claus.

There are no traditions of an annual gift-bringer in the Scandinavian countries. In the Orient, a small number of Christian groups have variants of Santa Claus that go by different names. Buddhist Japan, however, which has been eager for the past forty-five years to imitate American culture, has made Christmas a day of celebration—but not a work holiday. "Jingoru Beru" ("Jingle Bells") is played everywhere, and people wish one another a "Mari Kurisumasu." A few years ago I read in the *New York Times* that big department stores in Japan were dressing their elevator girl starters in miniskirted Santa Claus suits.

Papa Noël and Viejo Pascuero are, I am told, the Santa Clauses of Brazil and Chile respectively. They bring gifts from the South Pole on Christmas Eve, which in South America, of course, is the hottest time of the year. Canada, no doubt because of its proximity to the United States, has adopted Santa Claus entirely, except for French-speaking Quebec, where Père Noël is still the toy-bringer. In Australia, depending on where you live, it is either Santa Claus or Father Christmas who brings the gifts.

It was the Dutch settlers in New York, then called New Amsterdam, who brought Saint Nicholas to our shores, where his name was soon corrupted to Sint Klaes (also spelled Sinterklass, San Claas, and in other ways) and finally to Santa Claus. And it was Washington Irving who was the first to write about this. In his *History of New York* (1809), Irving reports that Dutch children would hang their stockings by the fire on St. Nicholas Eve (December 5), and the saint would come "riding over the tops of trees" in a "wagon" to send toys and candy rattling down the chimneys.

A Dutch ship sailed into New York Harbor with a wooden figurehead of Saint Nicholas—he was the patron saint of sailors—described by Irving as having "a low, broad-brimmed hat, a huge pair of Flemish trunk hose, and a pipe that reached to the end of the bowsprit." The Dutch settlers, he wrote, "built a fair and goodly chapel within the fort, which they consecrated to his [Saint Nicholas's] name; whereupon he immediately took the town of New Amsterdam under his peculiar patronage, and he has ever since been, and I devoutly hope will ever be, the tutelar saint of this excellent city." (All the above, by the way, turned out to be entirely fictitious.)

In Book 1, Chapter 5, of his history, Irving recounts a dream about Saint Nick that Moore must have seen since it describes smoke circling Santa's head and his gesture of putting a finger alongside his nose:

And the sage Oloffe dreamed a dream—and lo, the good St. Nicholas came riding over the tops of the trees in that selfsame wagon wherein he brings his yearly presents to children; and he came and descended hard by where the heroes of Communipaw had made their late repast. And the shrewd Van Kortlandt knew him by his broad hat, his long pipe, and the resemblance which he bore to the figure on the bow of the Goede Vrouw. And he lit his pipe by the fire and he sat himself down and smoked; and as he smoked, the smoke from his pipe ascended into the air and spread like a cloud overhead. And the sage Oloffe bethought him, and he hastened and climbed up to the top of one of the tallest trees, and saw that the smoke spread over a great extent of country—and as he considered it more attentively, he fancied that the great volume of smoke assumed a variety of marvelous forms, where in dim obscurity he saw shadowed out palaces and domes and lofty spires, all which lasted but a moment and then faded away, until the whole rolled off and nothing but the green woods were left. And when St. Nicholas had smoked his pipe, he twisted it in his hatband, and laying his finger beside his nose gave the astonished Van Kortlandt a very significant look; then mounting his wagon he returned over the tree tops and disappeared.

Moore's poem was the second major influence on the evolving American Santa. Having Saint Nick come down the chimney in person was probably Moore's invention. Of course, only a small person could do that, and for this reason Moore's Santa is a "jolly old elf" who arrives on a sleigh pulled by "tiny reindeer." Early pictures of Santa show him small. Even as late as 1902, when William Wallace Denslow, the illustrator of L. Frank Baum's *The Wonderful Wizard of Oz*, illustrated Moore's poem, he drew Santa as a little elf. It was also Moore who gave Santa his twinkling eyes, rosy cheeks, nose like a cherry, little round belly, and a large pack of toys.

"The sleigh drawn by reindeer was pure invention!" exclaims Stevenson. This was widely believed until it was discovered that in 1821, a year before Moore wrote his masterpiece, a small hand-colored book of eight pages and eight pictures was published in New York by William B. Gilley, a friend and neighbor of Moore. It was titled *The Children's Friend: Number III. A New-Year's Present to the Little Ones from Five to Twelve*. No author's name is on the booklet, but it is now known to have been both written and illustrated by Arthur J. Stansbury, a Presbyterian minister. It is the earliest known Christmas book printed in the United States. One of its pages shows Santa in a sleigh pulled by a single reindeer. Underneath are these lines:

Santa and his reindeer, from
The Children's Friend, *1821*

> Old Santeclaus with much delight
> His reindeer drives the frosty night
> O'er chimney tops, and track of snow
> To bring his yearly gifts to you.

It is hard to believe that Moore did not see this booklet before he introduced reindeer into his poem. Did the Reverend Arthur Stansbury invent the sleigh and reindeer? No one knows. It is possible that both sleigh and reindeer were part of the Dutch folklore about Saint Nick, though it was probably Moore who put the number of reindeer at eight.

Almost all fiction and verse published for children in England and America before 1800, with the exception of anonymous jingles like the Mother Goose rhymes, were didactic—intended to teach something, especially moral and religious values. I am indebted to Betsy Shirley for suggesting that not only was Moore's ballad the first American poem for children that has lasted; it also may have been the nation's first significant non-didactic poem for children.

The third great molder of Santa Claus was the cartoonist Thomas Nast (1840–1902), a German-born New Yorker who became famous for his attacks on the Tammany Tiger, a beast Nast created to symbolize New York City's corrupt political system presided over by Tammany Hall's "Boss" William Marcy Tweed. Nast also invented the donkey and elephant as symbols of our two major political parties. His first sketch of Santa appeared in *Harper's Weekly*, January 3, 1863, and from then until 1900 scarcely a Christmas went by without a Nast Santa in *Harper's Weekly*. Around 1869 Nast did full-color illustrations for an edition of Moore's poem published by McLoughlin Brothers.

Nast's earliest pictures of Santa show him small enough to go down chimneys, but in later Nast drawings he appears to be of normal height or even larger. He is always fat and jolly with a white beard. Nast replaced the all-fur coat Moore had given Santa with a red satin suit trimmed with white ermine. The pointed stocking cap, buckled shoes, and wide belt were other Nast touches. It was also Nast who gave Santa a home and workshop at the North Pole, and a large

book in which he records the names of children who have
behaved well throughout the year. Some of Nast's pictures
show Santa answering phone calls from children and reading
letters in which they request certain toys. The only Nast
touch that did not survive was the sprig of mistletoe he
always put on top of Santa's cap.

Hundreds of short stories and many novels have been
written about Santa. Mrs. Claus seems to have made her first
appearance in *Goody Santa Claus on a Sleigh Ride*, an 1899 novel
by Katherine Lee Bates. Bates was a popular novelist in her
day, but is now remembered only as the composer of "Amer-
ica the Beautiful." In my opinion, the best novel about Saint
Nick is *The Life and Adventures of Santa Claus* by L. Frank Baum

of Oz fame. Baum locates Santa in the Forest of Burzee, not far from Oz. The book explains how the gods of the forest reward Santa's goodness by conferring upon him the Mantle of Immortality.

It has become customary these days to complain about how early American Christmases, and the happy Christmases of Charles Dickens, have become corrupted by tasteless contemporary greed. For a growing number of families, the days preceding Christmas are now days of anxiety and depression. Yuletide Blues, as they have been called, are responsible for a rise in suicides that seems to peak during the period between December 25 and January 1. In big cities, the Christmas Blues are especially harsh on those who live alone, and on the thousands of homeless.

Things are not much better among well-to-do families. Like Thanksgiving, Christmas has degenerated into a holiday on which we gorge ourselves with fattening food, unmindful of the millions dying of starvation throughout the world. Traffic deaths in the nation increase by the hundreds as more people take to the roads, often under the influence of alcohol or drugs. Wild office parties have become such drunken saturnalias that many firms ban them.

Weeks before Thanksgiving, department stores now launch their seasonal orgy of hawking gifts that nobody needs and may not even want. Each year parents feel obligated to spend more and more on toys for children whose demands are intensified by television commercials that are often highly deceptive. To add to the annoyance, large toys often require complicated assembling according to opaque instructions, using screws and bolts that are sometimes missing or don't fit. A week later, most children have grown tired of their new possessions.

"Forgive us our Christmases," wrote Carolyn Wells, whose humorous verse included relentless attacks on Yuletide commercialism, "as we forgive those who Christmas against us."

Christmas lasted only a few days in Dickens's time, Russell Baker pointed out in a 1976 *New York Times* column, but "nowadays it persists like an onset of shingles. You spend a month getting ready for it and two weeks getting over it. . . . If Scrooge . . . had started dreaming on November 25 and spent the next four weeks being subjected to desperate sales clerks and electronically amplified 'Jingle Bells,' he probably would have stopped at the Cratchits' on that fateful evening only long enough to smash Tiny Tim's little crutch."

Commercialism has so overwhelmed the story of the birth of Jesus that some fundamentalist churches today oppose the celebration of Christmas. Early Calvinists in Europe and England and our own pre-Revolutionary Puritans were similarly offended by Yuletide shenanigans. Salem, Massachusetts, actually passed a law in 1628 banning the celebration of Christmas as a "wanton Bacchanalian feast. . . . God's time must not be frittered away." And today, three of our largest fundamentalist sects—the Seventh-Day Adventists, Jehovah's Witnesses, and the Worldwide Church of God—openly resist any celebration of it. For some fundamentalists, Christian Christmases are the work of Satan himself. In 1989 my son Tom was handed a tract issued by a nondenominational firm in Bennett, North Carolina, that bitterly denounced Santa Claus. Santa is shown on the tract's front page in a red suit, with horns on his head, a red tail, and a pitchfork in hand. Inside, we are told that "by the early eighteen hundreds Christmas had become so idolatrous that the American poet Clement C. Moore decided to take Christ completely out; by putting Santa in his sacrilegious poem, 'The Night Before Christmas,' and thus placing Santa on the Christmas throne and Christ in the cradle." Accompanying these sentiments is an anonymous five-stanza poem titled "Ho! Ho! Ho!" It begins:

> The devil has a demon,
> His name is Santa Claus.
> He's a dirty old demon.
> Because of last year's flaws.
> He promised Jack a yo-yo,
> And Jill a diamond ring.
> They woke up Christmas morning
> Without a single thing.

And ends:

One day they'll stand before God
Without their bag of tricks.
Without their red-nose reindeers,
Or their phony Old Saint Nicks;
For Revelation twenty-one,
Verse eight, tells where they'll go;
Condemned to everlasting hell,
Where there'll be no Ho! Ho! Ho!

I'm surprised that the author of this tract failed to observe that the letters of SANTA can be rearranged to spell SATAN!

It would be interesting to know how many parents today tell their small children that the Santa Claus in whose lap they sit for a photograph is the real thing, and how many explain that he is just someone dressed like Santa. The poor child must surely be confused if he or she is taken to more than one shopping mall, each with its own Santa, and then sees other Santas on sidewalks clanging bells for the Salvation Army. This leads to a question about which I have no firm opinion. Is it good or bad to let children believe in Santa Claus?

There are persuasive arguments on both sides. Parents

who think it is bad maintain that it is never good to tell children lies. When children learn the truth about Santa, they will find it harder to believe other things their parents tell them. A religious parent can argue that, after finding out Santa isn't real, a child will naturally conclude when he is older that God, too, isn't real—only a mythological figure to go alongside such cultural icons as Saint Nick and Uncle Sam.

On the other hand, it can be argued that children adore fantasy and derive enormous pleasure from the Santa Claus myth. True, they soon learn that the old fellow is a fraud, but this is harmless disenchantment. Moreover, children who are told there is no Santa come in conflict with believing pals if they try to reveal to them the awful truth. If you are a secular humanist (a popular euphemism for atheist) you can argue that letting children swallow the myth for a brief time is good training for becoming adult skeptics about God and Jesus. After all, the great Biblical miracles strain credulity even more than the story of a fat man who comes down chimneys and enters millions of houses in a single night.

British-born Robert Service (1875–1958), in *Rhymes of a Rolling Stone,* has a short poignant poem titled "The Skeptic" that goes like this:

> My Father Christmas passed away
> When I was barely seven.
> At twenty-one, alack-a-day,
> I lost my hope of heaven.
>
> Yet not in either lies the curse:
> The hell of it's because
> I don't know which loss hurt the worse—
> My God or Santa Claus.

Gamaliel Bradford's essay, "Santa Claus: A Psychograph," is a spirited defense of keeping the Santa myth alive among children. His final paragraph is worth quoting:

So the legend of Saint Nicholas is a lovely and delectable myth, the last living relic of the vanishing world of dreams. The fairies are gone. No little children or innocent maidens watch any longer through the ardent summer nights to catch some echo of the songs and dances of tiny people, footing it daintily over the dewy turf. The witches are gone. Unpleasant old ladies can look about them ill-favoredly and purvey gossip without the danger of being burned at the stake. Nobody pays heed to them and nobody fears what they do. The ghosts are gone. Solitary graveyards are far more comfortable and agreeable sojourning places in the summer evenings than crowded streets where one has to be constantly on the watch against becoming a ghost oneself. Santa Claus alone still lingers with us. For Heaven's sake, let us keep him as long as we can. There are some excellent people who are scrupulous about deceiving their children with such legendary nonsense. They are mistaken. The children learn to see soon enough, too clearly and too well, or to think they do. Ah, leave them at least one thrill of passionate mystery that may linger with them when the years begin to grow too plain and dull and bare. After all, in this universe of ignorance, anything may be true, even our dreams.

And there is a still deeper value in the preservation of the Santa Claus legend, even by those who have no faith in that or any other legend whatever. For such preservation typifies the profound principle that, sacred as both are, the law of love is higher than the law of truth. For this there is a perfectly simple and unassailable reason, that truth at its best is deceiving, but love is never. We toil and tire ourselves and sacrifice our lives for the dim goddess Truth. Then she eludes us, slips away from us, mocks at us. But love grows firmer and surer and more prevailing as the years pass by.

Therefore, why should not old and young alike, in the brilliant, deceptive Christmas moonlight, hearken for the tinkling bells and the pawing reindeer and echo the merry greeting of the saint, broadcast to the whole wide world:

"Merry Christmas to all and to all a good-night."

I happen to be a philosophical theist, so let me toss out a suggestion surely made before, though I have not encountered it. "Great believers," Thornton Wilder liked to say, "are great doubters." It's a poor faith that can't preserve itself in the face of evidence which seems to point toward foolishness. Perhaps allowing children to believe in Santa Claus, then later telling them that Santa doesn't exist, is a healthy preparation for adult trust in a power higher than imaginary gods and devils. A faith that can be damaged by early disenchantment over Santa Claus surely is not much of a faith.

TWO

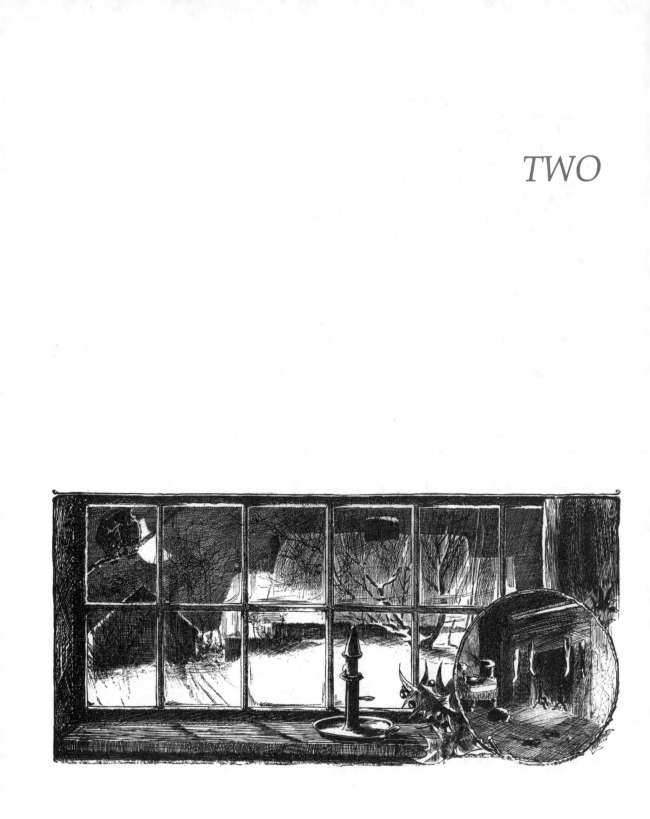

A VISIT FROM ST. NICHOLAS

by
Clement Clarke Moore

'Twas the night before Christmas, when all through the
    house
Not a creature was stirring, not even a mouse;
The stockings were hung by the chimney with care,
In hopes that St. Nicholas soon would be there;
The children were nestled all snug in their beds,
While visions of sugar-plums[1] danced in their heads;
And Mama in her 'kerchief,[2] and I in my cap,

1. Sugar-plums are sugar candy, or bonbons, in the form of small round
or flattened balls. Sugar-plum fairies dance in Tchaikovsky's Nutcracker
Ballet. Although Moore did not have them in mind, there actually are
sugared plums. They are made from plums grown in southern Portugal
and have been imported to the United States since 1875.
2. Kerchief: a square or rectangular piece of cloth that is folded, then tied
or pinned around the head and shoulders. Before houses were heated
with furnaces, it was a common practice to wear kerchiefs and caps to
keep the head warm on freezing winter nights.

Had just settled our brains for a long winter's nap;
When out on the lawn there arose such a clatter,
I sprang from the bed to see what was the matter.
Away to the window I flew like a flash,
Tore open the shutters and threw up the sash.
The moon on the breast of the new-fallen snow
Gave the luster of mid-day to objects below,
When, what to my wondering sight should appear
But a miniature sleigh, and eight tiny reindeer,
With a little old driver, so lively and quick,
I knew in a moment it must be St. Nick.
More rapid than eagles his coursers they came,
And he whistled, and shouted, and called them by name:
"Now, *Dasher!* now, *Dancer!* now, *Prancer* and *Vixen!*
On, *Comet!* on, *Cupid!* on, *Donder* and *Blitzen!*[3]

3. Isaac Asimov, in his note on these names in *Familiar Poems, Annotated*, writes: "One hangover from the Germanic past is 'Donder and Blitzen,' which means 'thunder and lightning.' All the names are suggestive of liveliness and speed (even Cupid is a winged god) except for Vixen, which is the word for a female fox, or, by extension, for a shrewish female human being. It seems the one inappropriate name, but Moore needed a rhyme or near-rhyme for Blitzen, we might suppose."

Small town newspapers seldom print a long poem without a few typographical errors. Whether this was the case, or whether the lady who copied down Moore's poem made the mistakes, this is how the couplet read in the original Troy newspaper publication:

Now! Dasher, now! Dancer, now! Prancer, and Vixen,
On! Comet! on, Cupid! on, Dunder and Blixem;

To the top of the porch! to the top of the wall!
Now dash away! dash away! dash away all!"
As dry leaves that before the wild hurricane fly,
When they meet with an obstacle, mount to the sky,
So up to the house-top the coursers they flew,
With the sleigh full of toys, and St. Nicholas too.
And then, in a twinkling, I heard on the roof
The prancing and pawing of each little hoof—
As I drew in my head and was turning around,
Down the chimney St. Nicholas came with a bound.
He was dressed all in fur from his head to his foot,
And his clothes were all tarnished with ashes and soot;
A bundle of toys he had flung on his back,
And he looked like a peddler just opening his pack.
His eyes—how they twinkled! his dimples how merry!
His cheeks were like roses, his nose like a cherry!
His droll little mouth was drawn up like a bow,
And the beard of his chin was as white as the snow;
The stump of a pipe he held tight in his teeth,
And the smoke it encircled his head like a wreath;[4]
He had a broad face and a little round belly,
That shook when he laughed, like a bowlful of jelly.
He was chubby and plump, a right jolly old elf,
And I laughed when I saw him, in spite of myself;
A wink of his eye and a twist of his head
Soon gave me to know I had nothing to dread;

"Dunder" and "Blixem" are also the names given on the Troy *Sentinel* broadside. We know that Moore intended the names to be Donder and Blitzen because that was how he spelled them when he included the ballad in his book of poems, and in 1862 when he wrote out the poem in longhand, the manuscript of which is owned by the New York Historical Society.

4. Angela Carter (in her article "Is Santa Claus Really St. Nicholas, Or Just Some Jolly, Beery Old Elf?," *New York Times Book Review*, December 7, 1986) suggests adding here the following couplet to accommodate the poem to the Surgeon General's warning:

> And that explains why he was quite out of breath,
> So little he knew he was dicing with death.

He spoke not a word, but went straight to his work,
And filled all the stockings; then turned with a jerk,
And laying his finger aside of his nose,
And giving a nod, up the chimney he rose;
He sprang to his sleigh, to his team gave a whistle,
And away they all flew like the down of a thistle.
But I heard him exclaim, ere he drove out of sight,
"Happy Christmas[5] to all, and to all a good night."

5. The first known printing of the poem in which the last line was altered
to "Merry Christmas to all . . ." was *Visit from Saint Nicholas*, illustrated
by F. O. C. Darley (New York: Hurd and Houghton, 1862, and Cambridge:
Riverside Press, 1862). Because we habitually say "Merry Christmas and
Happy New Year,"almost everyone misremembers this line. Even Gam-
aliel Bradford, at the end of his essay on Santa Claus, misquotes the line.

THREE

NIGHTS AFTER CHRISTMAS

The Night After Christmas, I

by Anonymous

The earliest printing of this poem known to me is in a book titled *The Night Before Christmas, or Kriss Kringle's Visit, by Clement C. Moore, with other Christmas poems*. The illustrations are credited to "Nick," and the publisher is given as "Willis P. Hazard, at Kriss Kringle's Headquarters, 724 Chestnut Street, Philadelphia." According to Betsy Shirley, who provided a photocopy of the book, the date is believed to be 1856.

The poem has been reprinted many times, always with slight variations in punctuation and in a few of its words. I

45

came across a reference to it having appeared in *Godey's Lady's Book and Magazine*, December, 1861. A booklet I own titled *Christmas Day* (Porter and Coates, 822 Chestnut Street, Philadelphia, 1872) credits it to *Punch* (no date), which I assume is the early American periodical of that name, not the British *Punch*. A corrupted version appears in J. W. Shoemaker's *Best Selections for Readings and Recitations* (Philadelphia, 1880).

The version given here is the one from 1856. I made two changes: removing "up" after the word "tucked" in line 5, and "had" as the second word of line 22 from the end.

Many other "Night After" sequels tell about children who are sick from eating too much food and candy. To avoid duplicating this theme, I have not included such poems by the following authors:

M. E. Ssafold (are the two s's printer's errors?) whose poem is in an undated *Santa Claus Story Picture Book* (M. A. Donahue, circa 1890), and in several later pre-1900 books.

Robert Archer, a Richmond, Virginia, medical doctor, who wrote his sequel in 1866. Apparently it was not published until 1975 when The Attic Press, in Richmond, issued it as a tiny book. The edition was limited to sixty copies, with hand-colored pictures by Elinor Shell. The poem begins: " 'Twas the night after Christmas and all over town/ The nurses were running, some up and some down."

An anonymous author whose sequel I found in *The Night Before Christmas* (Chicago: W. R. Conkey Company, 1897). It tells of Dr. Brough's arrival in a sleigh to medicate the children. "And I heard him exclaim as he drove out of sight/ These feastings and candies make doctor bills right."

'Twas the night after Christmas, when all through the
    house,
Every soul was abed, and still as a mouse,
The stockings so lately St. Nicholas' care,
Were emptied of all that was eatable there,
The darlings had been duly tucked in their beds—
With very full stomachs and pains in their heads.
I was dozing away in my new cotton cap,

And Nancy was rather far gone in a nap,
When out in the Nursery arose such a clatter,
I sprang from my sleep, crying—"What is the matter!"
I flew to each bedside, still half in a doze,
Tore open the curtains and threw off the clothes,
While the light of the taper served clearly to show
The piteous plight of those objects below;
For what to the fond father's eyes should appear,
But the little pale face of each sick little dear,
For each pet that had crammed itself full as a tick,
I knew in a moment now felt like old Nick.
Their pulses were rapid, their breathings the same,
What their stomachs rejected I'll mention by name—
Now Turkey, now Stuffing, Plum Pudding of course,
And Custards and Crullers, and Cranberry Sauce,
Before outraged nature all went to the wall,
Yes—Lollypops, Flapdoodle,[1] dinner and all.
Like pellets, which urchins from pop-guns let fly,
Went figs, nuts and raisins, jams, jelly and pie.
'Till each error of diet was brought to my view,
To the shame of Mamma and Santa Claus too.
I turned from the sight, to my bed-room stepped back,
And brought out a phial marked "Pulv. Ipecac,"[2]
When my Nancy exclaimed—for their sufferings shocked
    her—

1. Today, *flapdoodle* means nonsense, but in Civil War times it was commonly used in the British sense of food that fools are said to eat. The following lines are from Frederick Marryat's English novel *Peter Simple* (Chapter 28):

"It's my opinion, Peter, that the gentleman has eaten no small quantity of flapdoodle in his lifetime."

"What's that, O'Brien?" replied I.

"Why, Peter, it's the stuff they feed fools on."

2. Ipecac: a drug made by pulverizing the root of the ipecac plant. It is used to induce vomiting. "Ep-pe, pep-pe, kak-ke!" is a charm recited by the Wicked Witch of the West in Chapter 12 of L. Frank Baum's *The Wizard of Oz*.

Don't you think you had better, love, run for the Doctor?
I ran—and was scarcely back under my roof,
When I heard the sharp clatter of old Jalap's[3] hoof.
I might say that I hardly had turned myself round,
When the Doctor came into the room with a bound.
He was covered with mud from his head to his foot,
And the suit he had on was his very worst suit;
He hardly had time to put *that* on his back,
And he looked like a Falstaff, half fuddled with sack.[4]
His eyes how they twinkled! Had the Doctor got merry?
His cheeks looked like *Port* and his breath smelt of *Sherry*,
He hadn't been shaved for a fortnight or so,
And the beard on his chin wasn't white as the snow.
But inspecting their tongues in despite of their teeth,
And drawing his watch from his waistcoat beneath—
He felt of each pulse, saying:—"Each little belly
Must get rid"—here he laughed—"of the rest of that jelly."
I gazed on each chubby, plump, sick little elf,
And groaned when he said so, in spite of myself;
But a wink of his eye when he physicked our Fred,
Soon gave me to know I had nothing to dread.
He didn't prescribe—but went straightway to work,
And dosed all the rest—gave his trousers a jerk,
And adding directions while blowing his nose,
He buttoned his coat—from his chair he arose,
Then jumped in his gig—gave old Jalap a whistle,
And Jalap dashed off as if pricked by a thistle,
But the Doctor exclaimed, ere he drove out of sight,
"They'll be well to-morrow—good night! Jones—good
    night!"

3. Jalap: here used as the name for the doctor's horse. Jalap was a common
laxative of the day obtained from the root of a plant imported from Jalapa,
Mexico.
4. Sack: a seventeenth-century English expression for strong white wines
imported from Spain. "Will't please your lordship drink a cup of sack?"
asks a servant in Shakespeare's *Taming of the Shrew*, Induction, Scene 2.

The Night After Christmas, II

by Julia Boynton Green

Robert Haven Schauffler reprints this poem, with no indi-
cation of a prior publication, in his book *The Days We Celebrate*
(Dodd, Mead, 1960).

'Twas the night after Christmas, and all through the house
We were paying each one for our Yuletide carouse.
I felt in my tummy a burden like lead
And visions of tumors careened through my head.
Martha tumbled and tossed, at last breathed with a sob,
"I've got 'pendicitis—I'm sure of it, Bob."

But it was not for long we could nurse our own aches,
Tumult rose on the air—Martha cried, "Goodness sakes!"
It was mouthing and screeching that made my flesh
        creep—
Brother Henry was spouting a toast in his sleep.

I hustled to shake him; 'twas cold as the dickens,
Then skipped back to blankets and bed, frozen stiff.
But the respite was brief for we heard in a jiff
The sound a hyena in fits might have made—
Like the howl of a banshee—Quoth I, "The plot thickens.
That's nightmare—poor Grandma!" I flew to her aid.

Coming back I saw Martha was ready to cry.
Then to add the last straw to our nocturnal cares
A small spook in pajamas stole stealthily by—
Little Ted, our somnambulist, trotting down stairs.

I need only add that from midnight till two
We were hushing a juvenile hullabaloo.
Papa in his prowler, mamma in her cap,
Sat each with a suffering kiddie in lap.

*Some*thing they had swallowed that didn't agree,
And we very near drowned them in hot ginger tea.

I swore, about sunrise, "It's not worth the price.
Believe me, *next* Christmas we dine on boiled rice!"

The Night After Christmas, III

by Julia Boynton Green

I have no information on Ms. Green. I found this poem in
Richard Haven Schauffler's *The Days We Celebrate* (1960).

"Twas the night after Christmas, and all through the flat
Not a creature was stirring, not even the cat;
When close at my side there arose such a wailing
I leaped from my dreams and with words unavailing
Endeavored to fathom my Mary's distress;
At last she was forced the weird truth to confess:
"O Jack! I am ruined forever, I fear,
I sent Aunt the workbag she sent *me* last year!"

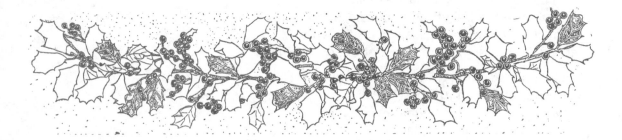

The Night After Christmas, IV

by Anne P. L. Field

This appears in Robert Haven Schauffler's anthology *Christmas* (Dodd, Mead, 1958). Can any reader tell me something about the author?

'Twas the night after Christmas in Santa-Claus land
And to rest from his labors St. Nicholas planned.
The reindeer were turned out to pasture and all
Ten thousand assistants discharged till the fall.
The furry great-coat was laid safely away
With the boots and the cap with its tassel so gay,
And toasting his toes by a merry wood fire,
What more could a weary old Santa desire?
So he puffed at his pipe and remarked to his wife,
"This amply makes up for my strenuous life!
From climbing down chimneys my legs fairly ache,
But it's well worth the while for the dear children's sake.
I'd bruise every bone in my body to see
The darlings' delight in a gift-laden tree!"
To make him think things were all coming out right,
For he didn't get one wink of slumber that night!
The telephone wire was kept sizzling hot
By children disgusted with presents they'd got,
And when the bright sun showed its face in the sky
The Santa-Claus family were ready to cry!
Just then something happened—a way of escape,
Though it came in the funniest possible shape—
An aeronaut, sorely in need of a meal,
Descended for breakfast—it seemed quite ideal!
For the end of it was, he invited his host
Out to try the balloon, of whose speed he could boast.
St. Nick, who was nothing if not a good sport,

Was delighted to go, and as quick as a thought
Climbed into the car for a flight in the air—
"No telephone bells can disturb me up there!"
Just then came a sound like a telephone bell—
Though why they should have such a thing I can't tell—
St. Nick gave a snort and exclaimed in a rage,
"Bad luck to inventions of this modern age!"
He grabbed the receiver—his face wore a frown
As he roared in the mouth-piece, "I will not come down
To exchange any toys like an up-to-date store,
Ring off, I'll not listen to anything more!"
Then he settled himself by the comforting blaze
And waxed reminiscent of halcyon days
When children were happy with simplest of toys:
A doll for the girls and a drum for the boys—
But again came that noisy disturber of peace
The telephone bell—would the sound never cease?
"Run and answer it, wife, all my patience has fled,
If they keep this thing up I shall wish I were dead!
I have worked night and day the best part of a year
To supply all the children, and what do I hear—
A boy who declares he received roller-skates
When he wanted a gun—and a cross girl who states
That she asked for a new Victor talking machine
And I brought her a sled, so she thinks I am 'mean!' "
Poor St. Nicholas looked just the picture of woe,
He needed some auto-suggestion, you know,
"And, wife, if it suits me I'll count it no crime
To stay up till ready for next Christmas time!"
Thus saying—he sailed in the giant balloon,
And I fear that he will not return very soon.
Now, when you ask "Central"[1] for Santa-Claus land
She'll say, "discontinued"—and you'll understand.

1. In the early days of the telephone, when you wanted someone's phone
number you asked for "Central," a telephone operator who gave such
information.

The Night After Christmas, V

by N. E. G.

I found this in typescript form in the Kellam Collection, at
the University of North Carolina, Chapel Hill. It was signed
only with initials, and no date or source was indicated.

'Twas the night after Christmas, and boy, what a house!
I felt like the devil, and so did the spouse.

The eggnog and turkey and candy were swell,
But ten hours later they sure gave me hell.

The stockings weren't hung by the chimney with care.
The darn things were sprawled on the back of a chair.

The children were nestled all snug in their bed,
And I had a large cake of ice on my head.

When at long last I dozed off in a nap,
The ice woke me up as it fell in my lap.

For some unknown reason I wanted a drink,
So I started in feeling my way to the sink.

I got along fine 'til I stepped on the cat.
I cannot recall what occurred after that.

When I came to, the house was all flooded with light,
Although under the table I was high as a kite.

While visions of sugar plums danced in my head,
I somehow got up and climbed back into bed.

Then what to my wandering mind should appear,
But a miniature sleigh and eight tiny reindeer.

Then the sleigh seemed to change to a mammoth fire truck,
And each reindeer turned into a bleary-eyed buck.

I knew in a moment it must be old Nick.
I tried to cry out, but my tongue was too thick.

The old devil whistled and shouted with glee,
While each buck pawed the earth and looked daggers at me.

Then he called them by name and the names made me shud-
    der.
When I heard them I felt like a ship minus rudder.

"Now Eggnog! Bacardi! Four Roes! and Brandy!
Now Fruit Cake! Cold Turkey! Gin Rickey! and Candy!

To the top of his house, to the top of his skull,
Now whack away, crack it with thumps that are dull!"

And then in a twinkling I felt on my roof
The prancing and pawing of each cloven hoof.

How long this went on I am sure I can't say,
Though it seemed an eternity plus a long day.

*Christmas Gambols,
or A Kiss Under
the Mistletoe*

But finally the night after Christmas had passed,
And I found that I really could think straight at last.

So I thought of the New Year a few days away,
And I made me a vow that no tempter can sway.

I'm sticking to water, don't even want ice,
For there's nothing so tasty, or nothing so nice.

The night after New Year may bother some guys,
But I've learned my lesson, and brother, I'm wise.

You can have your rich food, and your liquor that's red,
But what goes to my stomach won't go to my head.

So here's "Happy New Year" to you one and all.
I'm back on the wagon. I hope I don't fall.

The Night After Christmas, VI

by H. I. Phillips

Harry Irving ("Hi") Phillips was a nationally syndicated newspaper columnist who died in 1965, aged seventy-seven, in his hometown of Milford, Connecticut. He began his career as a reporter for the *New Haven Register* and later became its managing editor. His first column, "The Globe Trotter," appeared daily in the old *New York Globe*. When the *Globe* merged with the *New York Sun* in 1923, Phillips took over a column called "The Sun Dial." At the time of his death, his column, "The Once Over," was distributed by the Bell-McLure syndicate. Phillips also wrote several books about a World War II private he called Oscar Purkey.

I am told that this parody first appeared in Phillips's *New York Sun* column, December 26, 1935.

'Twas the night *after* Christmas, and all through the home
Raged a terrible headache wherever you'd roam.

The house looked a wreck. There were signs everywhere
To prove to the world that St. Nick had been there.

The children were still having fun with their toys,
And breaking all records for long-sustained noise,

When out in the hall there arose such a clatter,
I opened the door to see what was the matter.

And what to my wondering eyes should appear,
But a man in distress and devoid of good cheer.

He lay on the floor of the corridor narrow,
And out of the small of his back stuck an arrow!

It had come from the bow of his own little lad.
I knew in a moment it must be poor dad!

I rushed for the phone, and had just turned around
When mother crashed into the room with a bound,

Pursued by a child with a rifle. Oh, well,
It seems that to please him she played William Tell.

The apple was okay, but mother was not.
There wasn't a shadow of doubt she'd been shot.

The kid was still shooting his air gun—how merry!
He yelled, "Play some more, ma! It's funny, ma, very!"

Behind him came Willie, the boy from next door.
He carried a sword and he yelled, "Let's play war!"

He rode on a broom, took a wild swing at me
And carved quite a strip from the cap of my knee.

Then out of his room tottered old Uncle Lew,
His arm in a sling and one leg, I think, too.

He'd helped little Oscar try out his new sled,
And had quite a gash on the top of his head.

He'd also been playing with Ethelbert's skis,
And murmured quite weakly, "The ambulance, please!"

Next grandpa came wallowing out of the bath
(I never had seen any man in such wrath).

He looked all awash. He was all dripping wet.
His clothes were all soused. He was angry, you bet!

It served him quite right. Any man is a dub
When he tries to sail children's toy boats in the tub!

I stood there aghast when, no fooling, Aunt Nell
Swooped through on a kiddy-car, going pell-mell.

She upset the tree. There were sparks from a wire.
I knew in an instant the house was on fire!

Then things went all black, and when next I came to,
I was out on the lawn with a pullmotor crew.

The house was still burning, the kids, little dears!
Were dancing and shouting, and giving three cheers.

The fire chief stood by and completed his work.
He snickered a bit, then he turned with a jerk.

Laying a finger aside of his nose,
And, giving a nod, he said, "Roll up the hose!"

He jumped in his car, sounded siren and whistle,
And away he then flew like the down from a thistle.

And I heard him exclaim to his smoke-eating boys,
"Well, adults *will* play with the kids' Christmas toys!"

The Night After Christmas, VII

by Mrs. John T. Van Sant

This poem appeared in *St. Nicholas*, January 1915, sur-
rounded by a border illustration of broken toys. I was not
able to learn anything about the author.

'Twas the night after Christmas, and all through the house
Not a creature was stirring, not even the mouse!
The mechanical mouse, the marvelous mouse,
Who had traveled and traveled all over the house.

His spring was demolished, and powerless to run
From the little tin soldier with the little tin gun.
He lay on the hearth-rug and trembled with fear
Of the cotton-wool cat who was frightfully near—

The mechanical cat, so gaunt and so gray,
Who had chased him about on that same Christmas day.
And the little toy dog whose bark was controlled
By a spring in his side looked ferocious and bold

To the poor little mouse, the mechanical mouse,
Who had traveled and traveled all over the house.
In terror he shrank from the beasts in the zoo,
But he need not have feared. *Their* springs were smashed
   too!

FOUR

OTHER BALLADS AND SEQUELS

Annie and Willie's Prayer

by Sophia P. Snow

This sentimental poem appears anonymously, with slight textual differences, in many pre-1900 books. I have adopted the version in *Gems for the Fireside* (1883), a 912-page anthology edited by the Rev. O. H. Tiffany, published by A. W. Mills, Tecumseh, Michigan.

John Foster Kirk, in his *Supplement to Allibone's Critical Dictionary of English Literature and British and American Authors* (Lippincott, 1891) has an entry on Sophia P. Snow which reads (in full): "Annie and Willie's Prayer, Illust. London, 1884, 4to."

'Twas the eve before Christmas. "Good night," had been
  said,
And Annie and Willie had crept into bed;
There were tears on their pillows, and tears in their eyes,
And each little bosom was heaving with sighs,
For tonight their stern father's command had been given
That they should retire precisely at seven—
Instead of at eight—for they troubled him more
With questions unheard of than ever before:
He had told them he thought this delusion a sin,
No such creature as "Santa Claus" ever had been.
And he hoped, after this, he should never more hear
How he scrambled down chimneys with presents each year.
And this was the reason that two little heads
So restlessly tossed on their soft, downy beds.

Eight, nine, and the clock on the steeple tolled ten,
Not a word had been spoken by either till then,
When Willie's sad face from the blanket did peep,
And whispered, "Dear Annie, is 'ou fast as'eep?"
"Why no, brother Willie," a sweet voice replies,
"I've long tried in vain, but I can't shut my eyes,
For somehow it makes me so sorry because
Dear papa has said there is no 'Santa Claus.'
Now *we* know there is, and it can't be denied,
For he came every year before mamma died;
But, then, I've been thinking that she used to pray,
And God would hear everything mamma would say,
And maybe she asked Him to send Santa here
With that sackful of presents he brought every year."

"Well, why tan't we p'ay dest as mamma did den,
And ask Dod to send him with p'esents aden?"
"I've been thinking so too," and without a word more
Four little bare feet bounded out on the floor,
And four little knees the soft carpet pressed,
And two tiny hands were clasped close to each breast.
"Now, Willie, you know we must firmly believe
That the presents we ask for we're sure to receive;
You must wait very still till I say the 'Amen,'
And by that you will know that your turn has come then."

"Dear Jesus, look down on my brother and me,
And grant us the favor we're asking of thee.
I want a wax dolly, a tea set, and ring,
And an ebony workbox that shuts with a spring.
Bless papa, dear Jesus, and cause him to see
That Santa Claus loves us as much as does he;
Don't let him get fretful and angry again
At dear brother Willie and Annie. Amen."
"Please, Desus, 'et Santa Taus tum down tonight,
And b'ing us some p'esents before it is light;
I want he should div' me a nice 'ittle s'ed,
With bright shinin' 'unners, and all painted red;
A box full of tandy, a book, and a toy,
Amen, and then, Desus, I'll be a dood boy."

Their prayers being ended, they raised up their heads,
With hearts light and cheerful, again sought their beds.
They were soon lost in slumber, both peaceful and deep,
And with fairies in dreamland were roaming in sleep.

Eight, nine, and the little French clock had struck ten,
Ere the father had thought of his children again:
He seems now to hear Annie's half-suppressed sighs,
And to see the big tears stand in Willie's blue eyes.
"I was harsh with my darlings," he mentally said,
"And should not have sent them so early to bed;
But then I was troubled; my feelings found vent,
For bank-stock today has gone down ten per cent.
But of course they've forgotten their troubles ere this,

And that I denied them their thrice-asked-for kiss:
But, just to make sure, I'll steal up to their door,
For I never spoke harsh to my darlings before."
So saying, he softly ascended the stairs,
And arrived at the door to hear both of their prayers;
His Annie's "Bless papa" drew forth the big tears,
And Willie's grave promise fell sweet on his ears.
"Strange—strange—I'd forgotten," said he with a sigh,
"How I longed when a child to have Christmas draw nigh."
"I'll atone for my harshness," he inwardly said,
"By answering their prayers ere I sleep in my bed."
Then he turned to the stairs and softly went down,
Threw off velvet slippers and silk dressing gown,
Donned hat, coat, and boots, and was out in the street,
A millionaire facing the cold, driving sleet!
Nor stopped he until he had bought everything
From the box full of candy to tiny gold ring;
Indeed, he kept adding so much to his store,
That the various presents outnumbered a score.

Then homeward he turned. When his holiday load,
With Aunt Mary's help, in the nursery was stowed.
Miss Dolly was seated beneath a pine tree,
By the side of a table spread out for her tea;
A workbox well filled in the center was laid,
And on it the ring for which Annie had prayed,
A soldier in uniform stood by a sled
"With bright shining runners, and all painted red."
There were balls, dogs, and horses, books pleasing to see,
And birds of all colors were perched in the tree!
While Santa Claus, laughing, stood up in the top,
As if getting ready more presents to drop.

Now as the fond father the picture surveyed,
He thought for his trouble he had amply been paid,
And he said to himself, as he brushed off a tear,
"I'm happier tonight than I've been for a year;
I've enjoyed more true pleasure than ever before;
What care I if bank stock falls ten per cent more!
Hereafter I'll make it a rule, I believe,
To have Santa Claus visit us each Christmas Eve."

So thinking, he gently extinguished the light,
And, tripping down stairs, retired for the night.

As soon as the beams of the bright morning sun
Put the darkness to flight, and the stars one by one,
Four little blue eyes out of sleep opened wide,
And at the same moment the presents espied;
Then out of their beds they sprang with a bound,
And the very gifts prayed for were all of them found.
They laughed and they cried, in their innocent glee,
And shouted for papa to come quick and see
What presents old Santa Claus brought in the night
(Just the things that they wanted,) and left before light:
"And now," added Annie, in a voice soft and low,
"You'll believe there's a 'Santa Claus', papa, I know";
While dear little Willie climbed up on his knee,
Determined no secret between them should be,
And told in soft whispers how Annie had said
That their dear, blessed mamma, so long ago dead,
Used to kneel down and pray by the side of her chair,
And that God up in heaven had answered her prayer.
"Den we dot up and prayed dust as well as we tould,
And Dod answered our prayers: now wasn't He dood?"
"I should say that He was, if He sent you all these,
And knew just what presents my children would please.
(Well, well, let him think so, the dear little elf,
'Twould be cruel to tell him I did it myself.")

Blind father! who caused your stern heart to relent,
And the hasty words spoken so soon to repent?
'Twas the Being who bade you steal softly upstairs,
And made you His agent to answer their prayers.

Santa Claus's Petition

by Julie M. Lippman

This curious fantasy, in the form of a letter from Santa, appeared in the December 11, 1888, issue of *Harper's Young People*, a New York weekly periodical. Accompanying the poem was an illustration in color titled "Christmas Morning: A Hundred Fathoms Deep," by F. S. Church. I have no information about the artist or the author.

Dear children—I write in great haste just to say
I've met with an accident coming this way.

As Christmas is near, and I've so much to do,
I really must beg a slight favor of you:

And, unless I mistake, the small folks of this nation
Will spare poor old Santa great mortification

By setting about with their might and their main
To see that the accident's righted again.

You know, I suppose, that the distance is great
I travel each year: and for fear I'll be late,

I whip up my reindeer, and make each good steed
Go prancing along at the top of his speed.

This year my big sleigh was as full as't could hold:
I wrapped me up warm—for the weather was cold—

And started once more on my gay Christmas tour
With lightest of hearts, you may be very sure.

Hi! how the bells jingled and mingled in tune!
I bowed to the stars and I winked at the moon.

I found myself crossing the great open sea,
With dolphins and merchildren gazing at me.

I bent a bit over the side of my sleigh
To wave them a hand, when—ah, me! lackaday!—

A stocking crammed full to the very small toe
Fell over the back to the sea down below.

And there the merchildren made merry ado
With toys I had meant for some dear one of you.

So this is my accident, and I would ask—
I know you won't deem it a troublesome task—

That if you should see some poor child with no toys
Upon Christmas morning, dear girls and dear boys,

You'll know the fat stocking he was to have had
Is deep in the sea, and poor Santa is sad,

And see that the accident's righted, because
'Twill be a *great* favor to
Yours,

SANTA CLAUS.

A Letter to Kriss Kringle

by Anonymous

This poem may be short on aesthetic merit but it is long on
altruism. I found it pasted in an old scrapbook, circa 1883,
as a clipping from an undated, unidentified newspaper that
credited it to the *Chicago Tribune*.

Dear Kriss, I am puzzled by how you can fly
In a sleigh without wings and so high in the sky.
Sliding down chimneys through ashes and smoke,
Fur-covered Kriss, you're a regular joke.

How do you manage to carry such loads?
How do you manage to keep the right roads?

How do you know all the good girls and boys?
Why don't we wake with your clatter and noise?

How can you guess what we all would like best?
How can you please all the birds in the nest?
What are you doing the rest of the year?
Sleeping, I guess, with your little reindeer.

Oh, how I'd like to know true if you look
Jolly and fat, like the one in the book.
I'd keep awake but I know that you'd stay,
When children are watching, quite out of the way.

Kriss, when tonight you come round with a whirl
Don't forget Bessie, the washwoman's girl.
Bring something pretty, for last year, you know,
That was a chimney where you didn't go.

How does it happen you like the rich best,
Giving them much and forgetting the rest?
Kriss, that's all wrong, and it isn't the way.
All should be equal on Santa Claus day.

Kriss, good old Kriss, I'm afraid you'll be mad.
I only was joking. Don't put *me* down bad.
If Bessie's ma's chimney is crooked and small,
Never mind going to Bessie at all.

Bring up her playthings and put them with mine,
Wrapped with a separate paper and twine.
Soon as it's day, poor sick Bessie I'll see,
And give her the package you leave here with me.

After Santa Had Departed

by James Van Alen

In 1954 James Van Alen, a native of Newport, Rhode Island, who now lives in Greenville, New York, began an annual Christmas Eve reading of Moore's poem in the Newport house where Moore lived during his later years. Alen also founded what he calls The House of Santa Claus Society, which he hoped might some day buy the Moore home and turn it into a Santa Claus museum.

"When I was a kid," Alen told Charles D. Rice (who reported the interview in the Sunday newspaper supplement *This Week*, December 22, 1957), "I always thought the poem ended too soon. So I worked up a few more verses just to make the fun last longer. Besides, I used to worry about Father standing there by the open window as the poem closes. I was afraid he might catch cold, so now I've got him safely tucked into bed. I hope Dr. Moore isn't cross at me."

Mr. Van Alen began his yearly readings with his verse introduction to Moore's ballad, which is printed here, followed by the ballad and his postscript. The House of Santa Claus published Alen's two poems in 1958 in a booklet titled *A Christmas Eve Reading to the Children of America*. A cut version of the sequel was printed in Rice's interview.

 Dear children far and children near
The story you're about to hear

Was writ in eighteen twenty-two
For little children just like you

By Doctor Moore a kindly man
In whom the flow of poetry ran

So strong and true his verse and rhyme
Have stood the taxing test of time.

Yes, you tonight are going to hear
The age-old tale which year by year

'S been read in homes across the land
On Christmas Eve when hand in hand

Fond parents with their children sit
And read the pages only lit

By logs and candles burning bright
How Santa Claus will come tonight

And fill your stocking as he's done
For Father, Mother, everyone

Since once upon a time they too
Were little children just like you,

And then the story'll take a turn
And through another's lines you'll learn

What happy thankful thoughts went on
In Father's head when Santa'd gone.

So if you'll all sit very still
Your eyes and heads this tale will fill

With visions which on Christmas Eve
Are dreamt by all who do believe.

See! now the picture comes to life,
The Doctor, children and his wife
Are gathered that the tale be read
Before the children go to bed.

Postscript

I leant far out listening, my hands on the sill
No sound broke the silence, the night was so still,
'Twas hard to believe just one moment before
Saint Nick and his reindeer had raced past my door.

The air clear as crystal was frosty and crisp.
It turned the warm breath from my lips to a wisp
Of cottony cloud just as white and as thick
As the smoke from the short stumpy pipe of Saint Nick.

From the window I turned and to my surprise
Found Mamma and the children'd not opened their eyes.
But through the commotion'd continued to sleep
The slumber of innocents gentle and deep.

I eased down the sash with the greatest of care,
Refastened the shutters to foil the night air,
Then softly as wildly I'd sprung from my bed
Crept back, pulled the covers right up to my head.

To think that Saint Nick and I'd stood side by side
That of all on this Eve only I'd seen him ride!
Not the smallest detail must I let slip my mind,
For what'er I forgot would be gone with the wind.

So I lay snug and warm with the covers pulled high
While like troops on review each fresh mem'ry marched by
His swift flying team and his toy-laden sleigh
The moon on the snow turning night into day.

His lightness of foot and his quickness of motion
The prancing and pawing and sounds of commotion
The names of his coursers, the ash on his suit
His whistle shrill high and as clear as a flute.

His twinkle, his dimple, his nose like a cherry
His wink and his laugh none was ever so merry
My last fleeting view ere he drove out of sight
His friendly farewell "And to all a goodnight."

Then I thought, of the chimney I must take a view,
To make doubly sure what I'd witnessed was true,
And the fire's final flicker disclosed to my eyes
The stockings toy-filled stretched to three times their size.

Yes, Saint Nick had been here, it had not been a dream,
He had come and he'd gone like a phantom moonbeam,
But where moonbeams that vanish leave never a trace,
Clear proof of his visit hung by the fireplace.

As my eyes closed, I smiled at the wonder there'd be
In the morn when I told what had happened to me,
What questions and answers, what jumping and dancing
The picture I conjured was truly entrancing.

With my heart warm and happy, my night cap on tight
I resettled myself for the rest of the night
And I whispered so only the Good Lord would hear
"Bless my children, Saint Nick and his tiny reindeer."

St. Nick Visits a Salesgirl

by Harry Irving Phillips

For an identification of Phillips, see his "Night After Christmas" in the preceding section. This delightful parody probably first appeared in his widely syndicated newspaper column. It is reprinted in his book *On White or Rye* (Harper's, 1941).

'Twas the night before Christmas when all through the flat
Not a creature was stirrin' (include me in that);
My stockin's, a little the worse for the wear,
Was hung on the back of a three-legged chair;
Outside snow was fallin' in beautiful flakes,
But I didn't care—I was too full of aches;
I'd worked in a store through the holiday strife,
And was plannin' to sleep for the rest of my life,

When up from the airshaft there came such a clatter
I leaped out of bed to see what was the matter;
(I thought at the time 'twas a nut down one flight,
Who starts up his radio late ev'ry night);
So I went to the window and loudly did cry,
"Is this Christmas Eve or the Fourth of July?"

When what to my dead-with-sleep eyes did appear
But a hinky-dink sleigh and eight tiny reindeer!
And who should be drivin' right up to the door
But one of them masquerade guys from the store!
I said to myself, "What can be this nut's game?"
When he clucked to his reindeer and called 'em by name:
"Now Dasher! Now Dancer! Now Prancer! Now Vixen!
On Comet! On Cupid! On Donder and Blitzen!"
An' just as I'm dopin' what next he will do,
Right up to the housetop the whole outfit flew!

And then in a twinklin' I heard on the roof
The prancin' an' pawin' of meat on the hoof;
(Just imagine my feelings, with sleep nearly dead
And some sap with an animal act overhead!).
As I drew in my neck and was turnin' around,
Down the chimney my visitor came with a bound;
A big bag of junk he displayed with a grin,
And he acted to me like he'd like to move in.
He was chubby, good natured and oozin' with glee,
But I ask you, dear reader, what was it to me?
The point that I make is 'twas then 2 o'clock,
And a man in my room without stoppin' to knock!

I was thinkin' how noivy he was and how slick
When he says to me, "Lady, I'm only St. Nick."
Well, a poor tired store slave in no mood for fun,
I gave him a look and I asked him, "Which one?
As a Christmas rush salesgirl," I said, "you'll agree
That a look at St. Nick is no big treat to me;
This has gone far enough and this bunk's gotta stop—
Take the air with them goats or I'll yell for a cop!"

He spoke not word but went on with his work,
And filled up my stockin's, then turned with a jerk,
And layin' a finger aside his red nose,
And, givin' a nod, up the airshaft he rose. . . .
He sprang to his sleigh with a shake of his head,
And I pulled the shades down and fell into bed.
"Merry Christmas!" he called as away his deers flew,
And I just gave a yawn and I answers, "Sez you!"

The Booze Before Christmas

by Anonymous

I have several versions of this disgusting parody, no two
exactly alike. The one given here is essentially the same as
one that I found in a periodical called *The Launching Pad*
(December 1965), an eight-page newsletter that Arthur
Morje, a rare-book dealer in Philadelphia, used to mail to his
customers.

'Twas the night before Christmas, and all through the house
There were bottles and butts left around by some louse.

The fifth that I hid by the chimney with care,
Had been snatched by some bum who'd discovered it there.

My houseguests had long since been poured in their beds,
To wake in the morning with hungover heads.

My wife was out cold, with her chin on her lap,
And me, I was dying for one more nightcap.

When, through the north window there came such a smell,
I sprang to my feet to see just what the hell.

The moon, on the breast of the new fallen snow
Gave a luster of moonshine to objects below.

And what to my wondering eyes did appear
But a beer truck hitched up to eight drunken reindeer!

With a little old driver who looked like a hick,
But I saw it was Santa as tight as a tick!

Staggering onward those eight reindeer came,
While he hiccoughed and belched as he called them by name.

"On Schenley! On Seagram! We ain't got all night.
You too, Haig and Haig, and you too, Black and White.

Scram up to the roof. Get the hell off the wall.
Get going, you rummies, we've got a long haul!"

So up to the rooftop went reindeer and truck,
But a tree branch hit Santa before he could duck.

And then, in a twinkling, I heard from above,
A helluva noise that was no cooing dove!

As I pulled in my head and I cocked a sharp ear
Down the chimney came Nick, landing smack on his rear!

He was dressed all in furs, with no cuffs on his pants,
And the way the guy squirmed, I would swear he had ants!

His droll little mouth made him look a bit wacky,
And the beard on his chin was all stained with tobaccy.

He had nothing but booze in the sack on his back,
And a breath that would blow a freight train off its track.

He was chubby and plump, and he tried to stand right,
But he didn't fool me. He was high as a kite!

He spoke not a word, but went straight to his work,
Missing half of the stockings, the plastered old jerk!

Then putting his thumb to the tip of his nose
He gave me the bird. Up the chimney he rose.

He sprang for his truck at so hasty a pace
That he tripped on a gable and slid on his face.

But I heard him burp back as he faded from sight,
"Merry Christmas, you rum-bums, now go to sleep tight!"

The Effect of Inflation on Santa

by Dave Sharpe

This ably constructed parody, which comes to me by way of
Carolyn Fox, appeared in a periodical called *Tarnation*, De-
cember 1948.

'Twas the night before Christmas, and all through the house
How the tinsel was scattered! and twigs by the thous-
And. The stockings were hung by the chimney with
    care—
They were skewered with ten-penny nails, to be fair.
The children, God bless them, were snug in their beds,
With clothesline to anchor their ankles and heads.

The Wife in her housecoat, and I clad alike,
Had gone to the cellar to get the new bike,
When from a dark corner arose such a clatter
I felt a strong urge to forget the whole matter.

The wife said go over and open the door;
I grabbed a stout cudgel and crept 'cross the floor
And gingerly peered through the glass to behold
A wee red-suited man, turning blue with the cold.
Suppressing dire thoughts of a communist trick,
I flung wide the portal, admitting . . . St. Nick!

Poor Santa came in stamping snow from his feet
And cursing cold weather and all central heat:
"Your chimney's too small for a man of my girth"—
Which shows what the power of tradition is worth.
I asked him to stay, as the perfect host ought,
And my gimlet eyes gleamed at the parcels he brought.

Upstairs in the kitchen, hot toddy in hand,
Old Santa had both of us folks understand

That the new station wagon he'd purchased this year
To replace his eight quaint but archaic reindeer
Was the poorest investment he ever had chosen—
It stalled by our house with the engine plumb frozen.

My wife asked him then if the high cost of living
Had interfered much with the job of gift-giving.
"I'll say so," quoth he. "Why, a plain roller skate
Is costing me currently $10.98;
And the cheapest new belt, since inflation intruded,
Costs $4.27, all taxes included;
My labor is raising all manner of hob—
In fact, this here Christmas is too big a job."

He talked a while longer, but then had to go
When a wrecker from town came to give him a tow.
He left a tin whistle for Joey, our son,
And a watch for Matilda—I bet it won't run;
For the Wife, a new apron that makes her flesh crawl,
And a tie for yours truly completed our haul.
But I heard him exclaim, as he rolled out of sight,
"The blazes with Christmas—Tarnation is right!"

Santa Sells Out

by Carl Werner

This dated parody ran in the *Saturday Evening Post*, December 7, 1907. A reference to the Bronx suggests an apartment somewhere in Manhattan or Queens. I know nothing about the author.

'Twas the night before Christmas, when all through the
    flat,
Not a creature was stirring, not even a cat.

Above the steam heater our stockings were placed,
In hopes that by Santa they soon would be graced.

The children were snug in their wee folding beds,
While visions of Teddy bears danced in their heads.

And I in pajamas, likewise in a grouch,
Had gone to my patent convertible couch.

When out on the asphalt there rose such a clatter,
I sprang from my bed to see what was the matter.

A mantle of darkness enshrouded the room.
(The "quarter" gas meter had left us in gloom.)

But, after detaching a chair from my feet,
I threw back the curtain and looked down the street.

The arc light shone bright on our new garbage can,
Awaiting the call of the D.S.C.[1] man.

And what did my wandering optics devour,

1. D.S.C.: the first two letters probably stand for Department of Sanitation, but I have been unable to determine what the C stands for.

But a big touring car of a hundred horse power!

With a white-bearded driver, so shiny and slick,
I knew in a jiffy it must be St. Nick.

Like dry leaves before a wild hurricane fly,
He ascended the fire escape, nimble and spry.

I drew in my head and was turning around,
When down through the air shaft he came with a bound!

His coat was of broadcloth, the finest I've seen,
Though it smelled rather strongly of fresh gasoline.

A bundle of banknotes he had in a sack,
And he looked like a winner just home from the track.

His cheeks were like roses, his nose like a cherry.
He'd the air of a man who is satisfied—very!

A fragrant Perfecto he held in his teeth,
While its smoke crowned his ten-dollar tie like a wreath.

He had a broad face and a well-nourished belly
That shook when he laughed like a bowl full of jelly.

He was chubby and plump, but a shrewd little guy.
And there gleamed through his goggles a keen little eye.

He spoke not a word, but the foxy old elf
Just walked to the mantel and laid on the shelf

A letter typewritten in business-like style,
Then down the dumb waiter he sped with a smile.

He jumped in his car and with three loud "honk-honks,"
He whizzed 'round the corner and off toward the Bronx.

I opened the letter, the message I read,
And then I crept silently back into bed.

For here's what I saw, with dismay and disgust:
"Retired from business. Sold out to the trust."

A Modern Version of
The Night Before Christmas

by Robert McBlair

This parody of Moore's ballad was published in 1932, by the Press of the Wooly Whale, as a small book shaped like a cocktail shaker. The last page reads: "Contents of this shaker are guaranteed under the Food and Drug Act to be harmless and entirely legal. Dose: (for children) annual application; (adults) bottoms up." Below is printed: "Merry Christmas from Mr. and Mrs. Melbert B. Cary, Jr., 1932."

'Twas the night before Christmas,
  When all through the flat
Not a creature was sober,
  Not even the cat.
The glasses were placed
  On the mantel with care
In hopes that our Nicholas
  Soon would be there;
The children were dining
  At Tony's and Fred's
Where speakeasy vintages
  Danced through their heads;

And Mamma with her whiskey,
  And I with my gin,
Had just settled down
  For an evening of sin,
When out in the lane
  There arose such a clatter
I swallowed an olive—
  Now what was the matter?
A gulp to the window
  I fell like a flash,
Tore open the shutters
  And threw up the sash.

A light on the chest
  Of the new-fallen sleet
Gave a luster of mid-day
  To things on the street;
When what to my wondering
  Eyes should appear
But a truck loaded down
  With a mountain of beer,

And a little old driver,
  So lively and quick,
I knew in a moment
  It must be our Nick!
More rapid than eagles
  His helpers they came,
And he whistled and shouted
  And called them by name:
"Now, Lefty! Now, Louie!
  Now, Alky and Witzen!
On, Conky! On, Chowder!
  On, Harry and Blitzen!
To the top of the house—
  Ring the bells in the hall!
Now dash away, dash away,
  Dash away all!"

As dry leaves that before
  The wild hurricane fly,
When they meet with an obstacle,
  Mount to the sky,
So up to the top-floor
  The helpers they flew,
With a lift full of treasure—
  And Nicholas, too.
And then in a twinkling
  I heard on the flags
The prancing and pawing
  Of bottles in bags.

As I drew in my head
  And was turning around
In the doorway our Nicholas
  Came with a bound.

" 'Twas the night before Christmas,
And all through the contained space . . ."

ALAN DUNN
ARCHITECTURAL RECORD
MAGAZINE
1953

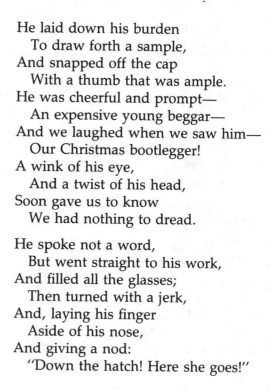

He was dressed like a Mayor
  From his head to his feet,
And his tie was all spangled
  With diamonds and sleet;
A bag full of beer
  He had flung on his back,
And he looked like a peddler
  Just opening his pack.

His rings, how they twinkled!
  His sniffle, how merry!
His hands were like roses,
  His eye like a cherry;
A scar drew his mouth
  To one side like a bow,
And the foam on his chin
  Was as white as the snow.
The gold of the dentist
  Was bright in his teeth,
And a derby encircled
  His head like a wreath.

He laid down his burden
  To draw forth a sample,
And snapped off the cap
  With a thumb that was ample.
He was cheerful and prompt—
  An expensive young beggar—
And we laughed when we saw him—
  Our Christmas bootlegger!
A wink of his eye,
  And a twist of his head,
Soon gave us to know
  We had nothing to dread.

He spoke not a word,
  But went straight to his work,
And filled all the glasses;
  Then turned with a jerk,
And, laying his finger
  Aside of his nose,
And giving a nod:
  "Down the hatch! Here she goes!"

He sprang to the door,
   To his men gave a whistle,
And away they all went
   Like the down of a thistle;

But I heard him exclaim
   Ere he drove out of sight,
"Happy Christmas to all,
   And to all a good night!"

Santa Changes His Mind

by Armand T. Ringer

Armand Ringer is the pseudonym of a minor poet who did
not want his identity disclosed. His sequel was written at
my request, and has not previously been in print.

It was months before Christmas, on August the first,
When millions were dying of hunger and thirst
In regions where food supplies couldn't keep pace
With oncoming hordes of fresh babies to face.

Up north, near the Pole, Santa tossed in his bed,
While visions of hopeless eyes glared in his head.
"Why should we," St. Nick asked himself with a sigh,
"Work so hard making toys that rich parents can buy?

"Each year the spoiled children keep begging for more
Of the marvels they see on display in the store.
Deceptive commercials play up to their greed
For electrical gadgets that none of them need.

"In America, Christmas occurs in December
To honor a birthdate, but who can remember
Whose birthday it is? Instead, it's a day
To eat, to imbibe, to be merry and play.

"I seem to recall a young sage who said, 'Do
Unto others as you'd have them do unto you.'[1]
Who hated the wealthy and told them to give
All their goods to the poor who were struggling to live.[2]

"I've decided next Christmas to alter my plans,
And instead of America, journey to lands
Where hunger is rampant. To hell with the toys.
I'll bring only *food* to the girls and the boys.

"To their parents I'll leave a big birth-control kit
With instructions on just how to do their own bit
To lower a birth-rate which year after year
Intensifies famines, diseases, and fear.

"For a decade or more I'll see what I can do
In Africa, Asia—in India, too.
And if parents can't learn to control their desire
For oversize families, I think I'll retire
(as my good wife has urged since the Roman Empire!).

"I'll offer my workshops to firms in Japan.
They make better toys than my laborers can.
If Japan doesn't want 'em, perhaps I can dump
All my elves and equipment on Turner or Trump.[3]

"I'll ship my nine reindeer to zoos where it snows,
Including dear Rudolph whose schnozzle still glows.
I'm getting too chubby—no topic for joking!
Shall I stop eating blubber and give up pipe smoking?

"We'll stay where we are, where there's plenty of room.
No hunger, no wars, no pollution, no gloom.
What I need most of all is a decade of rest
To relax, ignore T.V., and hope for the best.

"We'll catch up on reading, our greenhouses tend,
While we wait to see how old earth's history will end."

1. Matthew 7:12, Luke 6:31.
2. Matthew 19:21.
3. Ted Turner, who, among other things, owns the CNN cable television
network, and Donald Trump, the builder who at the time this was written
seemed to own half of Manhattan and Atlantic City.

Christmas on Mt. Olympus

by Carolyn Wells

Carolyn Wells (1869–1942) was a prolific, enormously popular writer of fiction (for both adults and children) and of humorous verse. Indeed, she was the nation's top woman humorist from 1900 to 1920. She also edited anthologies of verse: *A Nonsense Anthology*, *A Parody Anthology*, *A Whimsy Anthology*, and many others. Most of her mystery novels—there were more than seventy-five!—featured a sleuth named Fleming Stone.

The following parody is from her book of poetry, *Christmas Carollin'* (1913).

'Twas the night before Christmas; Olympia's height
Was ringing with laughter and blazing with light.
The gods and the goddesses (see Murray's Manual)[1]
Were holding their regular Christmas-Eve annual.
In the gorgeous Olympian dancing-pavilion
Apollo was leading the mazy cotillion,
When out at the gate there arose such a clatter,
The deities ran to see what was the matter.
There they found Santa Claus in a terrible plight,
His sleigh, heavy-laden, had broken down, quite.

Poor man! He had started in gladness and mirth
With his yearly consignment of presents to earth.
And now, each fair gift designed for a mortal
Was dumped on the ground at Olympia's portal!
But the gods and the goddesses generous are,
And Aurora said, "Santa, I'll lend you my car."
The offer was gladly accepted. Saint Nick
Transferred all his bundles surprisingly quick.

Then he said, "Your assistance is of such great worth

I'll bring you a beautiful present from earth.
Now if you and the others will mention, my dear,
Whatever you want that you can't get up here—"
"You love!" cried Aurora, with jubilant squeal.
"I'll take, if you please, an automobile!"
"You darling!" cried Venus, "pray bring me from town
A big picture hat and a new Paris gown."
"My order," said Mercury, "is roller skates."
Achilles said, "I'd like a pair of heel-plates."[2]
Fair Niobe sobbed, "Since I always must cry,
Of handkerchiefs bring me a goodly supply."
Said Laocoön, "They say whisky's a cure
For snakebite—if so, I should like some, I'm sure."[3]
"I'm not quite in form," said old Hercules,
"So I'd be obliged for a punching-bag, please."
Said Ajax, "A lightning-rod, sir, is my choice."
While Mars said a Krupp gun would make him rejoice.
Minerva (you know she's exceedingly wise)
Said a late Boston Transcript she greatly would prize.
Well, Santa Claus finally finished his list,
And said, "Is this all? Is any one missed?"
"Well, yes," Æsculapius said, "if you please,
I've encountered the old-fashioned forms of disease;
But my pupils and I think 'twould greatly delight us
If you'd bring us a patient with appendicitis."
"All right!" answered Santa Claus, "I shall obey.
Merry Christmas to all!" and he hurried away.

1. Alexander S. Murray's *Manual of Mythology*, a standard reference (revised second edition, 1888).
2. To protect his "Achilles' heel" of course.
3. Laocoön was a Greek priest of Apollo who warned the Trojans against accepting the wooden horse. The gods punished him by sending two sea serpents that killed him and his two sons.

Another Visit of St. Nicholas

by Carolyn Wells

This ballad by Carolyn Wells can be found in her book of
verse, *The Merry-Go-Round* (1901).

'Twas the day before Christmas, and all through the school
The pupils were restless and broke every rule.
A spirit of mischief pervaded the air,
And the master at last stamped his foot in despair.
He thumped on his desk, and he said, "Girls and boys,
Come to order at once. I won't have so much noise!
Attend to your lessons, and understand clearly,
The next one who speaks shall be punished severely."
Appalled by this threat, for a time no one spoke,
Until with a chuckle, suppressed to a choke,
"Please, sir," said the voice of the tiniest scholar,
"Tomorrow is Christmas, and I've got to holler!"
The pupils looked scared, and the master looked black.
He glanced at the birch rod that hung at his back.
But as he arose and was turning around,
Down the chimney St. Nicholas came with a bound.
He was dressed all in fur from his head to his foot,
And his clothes were all covered with ashes and soot.
"Merry Christmas, my children," he said, with a wink,
Then he turned to the master, and—what do you think?—
He looked at him queerly. "My dear sir," he said,
"You may go to your home, and I'll stay here instead.
Take your coat from the peg and your hat from the shelf.
The rest of today I will teach school myself."
The master departed. St. Nicholas took
His seat at the desk and he opened a book.
"Hoot, toot!" he exclaimed. "What nonsense is this?
I'll teach you some lessons worth learning, I wis.

And nothing today in this school must be taught,
But shall with the spirit of Christmas be fraught.
Put away all your books and just listen to me."
The children right gladly obeyed his decree,
And attentively sat, while St. Nicholas's lore
Made attractive the studies so stupid of yore.
The botany class he found easy to please
By a simple analysis of Christmas trees;
Their species and habits, their culture and use,
And the relative merits of hemlock and spruce.
Of the red holly berry and white mistletoe
He gave a description and told how they grow.
The history class learned that once on a time
Long, long years ago, in a far distant clime,
There dawned on this earth the first Christmas day,
And this class was well pleased to discover that they
Had no long string of difficult dates to remember.
They need learn only one—twenty-fifth of December.
The astronomy class was told of a star
That appeared long years since, in a country afar.
Then Nicholas said, "Children dear, if you please,

We will now sing some carols and catches and glees."[1]
The geography class then this queer teacher told
Of his far-away home at the North Pole so cold.
He described it, and then the obliging old chap
Turned round to the blackboard and drew them a map
To show them the route which he travels each year,
With his miniature sleigh and eight tiny reindeer.
The classes in science were then taught to know
The wonderful value of ice, frost and snow.
St. Nicholas chuckled while wisely dilating
On the process of snowballing, coasting or skating.
The geometry pupils were sent to the board,
And by diagrams made with a crayon and cord
Were taught to inscribe with an accurate eye
Component triangles in circles of pie.
A lecture on natural history then
The teacher announced as he laid down his pen.
And the pupils all listened, delighted to hear
Description and tales of the noble reindeer.
Ornithology followed, in well chosen words
Which made clear to them all that the principal birds,
The handsomest birds, and the birds of most use,
Without doubt are the turkey, the duck and the goose.
Physiology next, and the children learned why
It is best not to eat too much candy and pie.
Last of all came the class in industrial arts,
And by numerous diagrams, sketches and charts
St. Nick to the children, who round him were flocking,
Demonstrated the best way to hang up a stocking.
"Now lessons are over," St. Nicholas said,
"Skurry home, eat your suppers and hop into bed.
For until you are all wrapped in slumber profound
I cannot start out on my annual round."
He sprang to his sleigh and he reached for his whip.
The children ran home with a hop and a skip.
But they heard him exclaim, ere he drove out of sight,
"Merry Christmas to all! I will drop in tonight."

1. Glees and catches are unaccompanied songs for three or more voices.
Catches are so-called because they are more amusing, often with sugges-
tive lyrics. Glee clubs sing glees and other kinds of songs.

The Night Before Christmas

by Carolyn Wells

Like the previous poem, this appears in Wells's 1901 collection of verse, *The Merry-Go-Round.*

'Twas the night before Christmas, and all through the house
Everybody was sleeping as still as a mouse.
No stockings were hung and no presents prepared,
No Christmas-tree ordered,—but nobody cared;
Or at least no one seemed to be troubling himself,
No turkeys were killed, no mince pies on the shelf—
No bright-berried holly was wreathed on the wall,
No mistletoe bough had been hung in the hall.
'Twas surely the night before Christmas, and yet
Every one in the house seemed this fact to forget.
But this happened in Norway, so nothing was wrong,
For their night before Christmas is just six months long.

Christmas in Mothergooseland

by Carolyn Wells

Still another account of a visit by Santa Claus, from Wells's
The Merry-Go-Round.

A long time ago, in a land far away,
Mother Goose gave a party one bright Christmas-day.
She marshaled her children in brilliant array,
And invited the folk from Fairy-Tale way.
There was sweet Cinderella, Dame Trot and her cat;
And Jack the Giant-Killer, and Horner and Spratt.
There was Little Boy Blue,
And the Frog who would woo,
And the funny Old Woman who Lived in a Shoe.
There was Little Miss Muffet and Red-Ridinghood,
And Hop-o'-my-Thumb and the Babes in the Wood.

There was jolly King Cole
And his fiddlers droll,
And a great many more that I cannot enroll.
When all were assembled, so history tells,
They heard in the distance a chiming of bells,
And, drawn by his eight prancing reindeer so gay,
Santa Claus soon appeared in his glittering sleigh.
The children all gathered around him with joy,
And each one received a most beautiful toy;
And—this part of the tale you can scarcely believe—
Whatever they asked they were sure to receive.
Their gifts made them all as happy as kings,
But some of them asked for the funniest things.
The Babes in the Wood desired new winter suits.
Cinderella said she wanted high rubber boots.
And Little Boy Blue was longing, he said,
For a nice little bed,
With a blue-and-white spread,
And a soft feather pillow to put 'neath his head.
Jack Horner requested a silver pie-knife;
Jack Spratt said he'd like a new gown for his wife.
Then Jack and Jill said
That they wanted a sled,
With shining steel runners, and painted bright red.
Simple Simon announced he'd like turnover pies,
Of various flavors and rather good size.
Mother Hubbard remarked, in quavering tones,
That she'd be much obliged for a bushel of bones.
Bo Peep said she'd love to have a new crook;
The Queen of Hearts asked for a recipe-book.
And thus Santa Claus went on through the list;
Each had a fine present and no one was missed.
Then he jumped into his sleigh and drove out of sight;
"Merry Christmas," he called, "and to all a good night!"
And each guest went home saying, "This seems to me
The very best party that ever could be."

Santa Claus and the Mouse

by Anne Emilie Poulsson

Although this and the next two poems are not in anapestic
meter, and are not strictly sequels to Moore's ballad, I include
them in the hope that readers will enjoy them.

Miss Poulsson (1853–1939) was a blind, New Jersey-
born, kindergarten teacher who wrote many books for
children, and about the teaching of children. Her widely
anthologized poem about Santa and the mouse first appeared
in *St. Nicholas*, January 1884.

One Christmas Eve, when Santa Claus
   Came to a certain house,
To fill the children's stockings there,
   He found a little mouse.

"A Merry Christmas, little friend,"
   Said Santa good and kind.
"The same to you, sir," said the mouse,
"I thought you wouldn't mind,

If I should stay awake tonight
   And watch you for a while."
"You're very welcome, little mouse,"
   Said Santa, with a smile.

And then he filled the stockings up
   Before the mouse could wink—
From toe to top, from top to toe,
   There wasn't left a chink.

"Now they won't hold another thing,"
   Said Santa Claus with pride.
A twinkle came in mouse's eyes,
   But humbly he replied:

"It's not polite to contradict—
   Your pardon I implore—
But in the fullest stocking there
   I could put one thing more."

"Oh, ho!" laughed Santa, "silly mouse,
   Don't I know how to pack?
By filling stockings all these years
   I should have learned the knack."

And then he took the stocking down
   From where it hung so high,
And said, "Now put in one thing more.
   I give you leave to try."

The mousie chuckled to himself,
   And then he softly stole
Right to the stocking's crowded toe
   And gnawed a little hole!

"Now, if you please, good Santa Claus,
   I've put in one thing more,
For you will own that little hole
   Was not in there before."

How Santa Claus did laugh and laugh!
  And then he gaily spoke,
"Well! you shall have a Christmas cheese
  For that nice little joke."

If you don't think this story true,
  Why! I can show to you
The very stocking with the hole
  The little mouse gnawed through.

Kris Kringle's Surprise

by Henry Davenport

I found this amusing poem in *Crown Jewels or Gems of Literature, Art and Music* (Philadelphia: International Publishing Co., 1887), compiled by Henry Davenport Northrop. I know nothing about the author or his relationship to the compiler.

With heavy pack upon his back,
  And smiles upon his face,
Kris Kringle waded through the snow
  And went at rapid pace.
His sack that made him sweat and tug
  Was stuffed with pretty toys,
And up and down throughout the town
  He sought the girls and boys.

Not long before, within one door,
  One little Johnny Street,
By lucky chance got into pants,
  And grew about two feet.
On Christmas eve he asked for leave
  To hang upon a peg
The woolen stockings he had worn,
  Each with its lengthy leg.

The cunning boy, on Christmas joy
  With all his heart was bent,
And for old Kringle's packages
  With all his might he went.
In big surprise Kris Kringle's eyes
  Stuck out and stared around,
For two such stockings as those were
  He ne'er before had found.

He thought he'd never get them full,
  They were so strangely deep;
So, standing there upon a chair,
  He took a hasty peep:
Young Johnny Street, the little cheat,
  Had watched his lucky chance,
And to the stockings, at the top,
  Had pinned his pair of pants.

If Santa Is a Little Late Tonight

by C. P. Donnel, Jr.

In this poem we learn how swiftly Santa reacted when he received, from a little Russian girl, a letter that had been smuggled out of the Soviet Union—a land where Santa had been banished as a capitalist myth. The poem appeared in the *Saturday Evening Post*, December 27, 1952.

While Santa was shuffling his last-minute mail,
   He came on a note that was scrawled
In a faraway land, in a little girl's hand,
   In a language he hardly recalled.
Not an elf made a sound as he scanned it and frowned,
   Then he leaped to his feet with a shout,
And he held out the screed for his workers to read.
   "By Blitzen!" they cheered. "Smuggled out!"

Mrs. Santa said firmly, "This calls for a trip
   You must make up your mind to forgo.
With the reindeer and pack you're a setup for flak
   If you fly at a sensible low.
While their radar and planes make their stratosphere lanes
   Uncertain and hazardous channels;
You're too old."
Here the saint interrupted, "I ain't,
   And I'll thank you to fetch my red flannels.

"For a summons like this I have waited for years,
   While I smoldered continually with
The desire to shame certain people who claim
   I'm a decadent, capitalist myth.
Moreover, I'm riled that this resolute child
   Cannot openly send in her order.
Though I seldom intrude, I am now in the mood,
   Where I'll violate somebody's border."

He was ready to leave when his wife hurried up:
   "I have charted your route on this map.
Fly on oxygen, pray, for two-thirds of the way,
   And avoid the Siberian trap.
Then here, at this town, you will start to drop down
   Till you spot the great Petrovitch Dam.
Level off by degrees, and watch out for tall trees. . . .
   Are you listening?"
         Said Santa, "Yes, ma'am.

"Tell the world," Santa barked, "of my earnest request
   For no public excitement or fuss
If I'm tardy tonight. You may label this flight
   Operation Priority Plus.
I will show certain folks who's a fable and hoax."
   Then, as spry as a two-month-old pup,
He scrambled aboard, and he boomed as he soared,
   "One doll, extra large, coming up!"

Santa and the Cat

by Alice Byrne Pape

This pleasant account of the night before Christmas, as seen
by a house cat, is from *St. Nicholas*, December 1923.

The night before Christmas was frosty and still;
A blanket of snow lay on Hollyhock Hill;
And Rosemary Smithkins and Moppet and Ted
Had hung up their stockings and long been abed.

Their mother alone in the living-room sat—
That is, all alone but for Peter, the cat,
Who crouched on the hearth-rug, a spot he preferred,
With paws folded in as he toasted and purred.

The grandfather's clock on the stairs chanted ten,
Resuming its solemn tick-tocking, and then
A jingle of bells on the road far away,
Foretold the approach of a swift-moving sleigh.

The mother of Rosemary, Moppet, and Ted
Looked gravely at Peter. "There's Santa," she said.
"I think we'd both better retire for the night."
She picked up the pussy and put out the light.

Now every one else in the house was a-sleeping
When little fur Peter came downstairs a-creeping.
His paddy-paws made not a sound on the floor
As he cautiously stole toward the living-room door.

He peered round the edge, and a sight met his eyes
That caused him to hump up his back with surprise—
An evergreen tree decked in festive array
With garlands of tinsel and ornaments gay,

And, moving about with much haste, minus noise,

In the midst of a great helter-skelter of toys,
A fat little man in a jacket and hood
Was working away just as fast as he could.

Said the fat little man: "Here are snow-shoes for Ted;
For Moppet, this dolly asleep in a bed;
A desk set for Rosemary; gloves lined with fleece,
Three warm knitted mufflers, a sweater apiece;

"Some pictures to hang on the nursery wall,
A brand-new toboggan, a bat and a ball,
And handkerchiefs bordered in every hue,
And striped Christmas candies, and oranges, too."

When all of these things were arranged near the tree,
The spectacle truly was gorgeous to see.
Then up through the chimney, without more delay,
The fat little gentleman hastened away.

Fur Peter returned to the hearth-rug to keep
A vigil for mice; but he soon fell asleep.
When midnight rang out through the slumbering house,
No creature was stirring—not—even—a—mouse!

Santa's Surprise Party

by Gladys Hyatt Sinclair

A group of children turn the tables on Santa by bringing him
gifts, though how they manage to get to the North Pole and
back remains a mystery. I found this fantasy in *St. Nicholas*,
December 1908.

'Twas a glad Christmas eve, and all over the world,
With reindeer and sleigh dear old Santa had whirled.
No one was forgotten or slighted by him;
Each stocking was bulging and crammed to the brim.
"There!" cried the old saint as he stopped at his door,
"I've made all the little ones happy once more!
But the rest of the night will be lonely, I fear;
Why—what is this wonderful racket I hear?"
He bounded down nimbly, so great his surprise,
But stopped just inside, scarce believing his eyes;
For here were the children that he had supposed
Were sleeping down yonder with eyes tightly closed;
Here, singing and dancing and frisking in glee
Around a most dazzling and beautiful tree!
"Oh, Santa," they cried, "we have found you at last!
How tired you must be! You have journeyed so fast
To take us good gifts; but now, Santa Claus, see!
We have brought *you* some gifts, and this splendid, big tree!
We want you to know, just for once in a way,
How happy you make us, each new Christmas day.
These gifts did not grow in your Christmas tree grove;
We brought them for you, with our very best love!"
Then I wish you had seen them lead Santa about
To examine his gifts—heard his laugh and his shout
When he found a fur coat with a collar so wide,
When he read the gay note that was fastened inside!

There were bells for the reindeer, a pipe and red mittens,
And one little girl had brought Santa her kittens.
He'd a brush for his clothes and a brush for his hair,
He had pictures and books and a great easy chair
Where a good saint might nap it and sit at his ease

While presents grew ripe on his evergreen trees.
He'd a pair of new spectacles, shining and bright,
To help him to fill little stockings aright.
There were cushions so soft for the magical sleigh,
A cap trimmed with fur and a dressing-gown gay,
And stockings so long and so warm and so thick,
Jack Frost can no more play his favorite trick
Of blowing a blast upon Santa Claus' toes
As over the steeples, at Christmas, he goes.
"Please wear this red scarf!" whispered one little elf:
"I made it, dear Santa; I worked it myself!"
He caught up the girlie and gave her a kiss.
He hugged them and thanked them—not one did he miss;
Then, "laying his finger aside of his nose,"
He twinkled his eyes—and what do you suppose?
Such visions of stockings, filled up to the top,
Bedazzled those children, they scarcely could stop
To cry "Merry Christmas! Good night, Santa dear!"
And to wish him a glorious "Happy New Year!"

Then home o'er the cloud hills they scampered and ran:
Now guess all the gifts that they found—if you can!

Going My Way?

by Rolaine Hochstein

A New Jersey resident, Rolaine Hochstein is the author of two novels, *Table 47* and *Stepping Out*, as well as numerous short stories (perhaps the best known is "What Kind of a Man Cuts His Finger Off?"), articles, and poems that have won many awards. She also writes occasional travel articles

for the *Washington Post,* and has co-authored, with Daniel
Sugarman, Ph.D., three books for children and teenagers.
Her well-crafted parody of Moore's poem appeared in *Ms.*
magazine, December 1972.

'Twas the night before Christmas and, darling, don't ask.
Hercules would have collapsed at the task.
My head was in circles with so much to do
For a family of five and Saint Nicholas, too.
The house was a mess with the children so hearty
And Dad was delayed at his company party.
The kids danced around me proclaiming their wishes
While I was still up to my elbows in dishes.
And as I cleaned up from the little folks' dinners,
I wondered just what I would do for beginners:
I thought of the wrapping of gifts by the dozens,
Of cooking tomorrow for twenty-three cousins,
Of trimming the tree and of cleaning the house,
Of fixing a Bromo to give to my spouse,
Of shining the silver, the copper, the brass,
Of washing and rinsing and polishing glass,
Of strewing the tinsel and peeling tomatoes
And hanging the holly and mashing potatoes,
Of slicing the stringbeans and icing the tarts,
Combining the olives and celery hearts,
Of tossing the salad and baking the pies
And stretching the table to double its size.
The trays were prepared and the punch bowl was handy,
The brandied plum pudding was soaking in brandy.
The night was still young; I had nothing to dread,
But thoughts of catastrophe danced in my head:
The baby needs bathing, the cloth needs a pressing,
The rug needs a vacuum, the turkey needs dressing,
My hair needs a setting, the children are fretful,
And where is my husband and why so forgetful?
I was just on the border of losing my poise
When out on the lawn there arose a great noise.
Away through the doorway I flew on the double

Atremble lest hubby had tripped into trouble.
The lawn was as green as the first day in May;
We had not had a snowfall so how come the sleigh?
Instead of my husband, this cool little chap
In black leather boots and a plaid golfing cap,
With sideburns and moustache and velveteen vest
And a *Celebrate Life* button pinned on his chest.
His smile was so dapper, his bright eyes so gleaming
And was that a joint in his hand? Or me dreaming?
But when I caught on to the look in his eye
I knew it was Santa himself—flying high.
The reindeer were champing and chafing their bits
So quick as a flash, I collected my wits.
I saw there was room for one more in the sleigh
And I stuck out a thumb and said, "Going my way?"
Whereupon Santa Claus, with a mischievous grin,
Tossed out his toy sack and bade me, "Hop in!"
It was just what I needed: a Christmas vacation,
My very first flight into Mom's Liberation.
I sang a refrain as we sped from the sphere:
"Happy Christmas to all and I"ll see you next year."

FIVE

THE NEW YORK MAGAZINE COMPETITION

In December 1973, Mary Ann Madden, of *New York* magazine, sponsored a competition for eighteen-line parodies of Moore's poem. Winners were published in the December 23 issue. The three poems here won the first, second, and third prize respectively. For the eight amusing runner-ups, see the issue of *New York*, cited above, in which they were printed.

The Year Dickie Quit

by John Hofer

'Twas the night before Christmas, the year Dickie[1] quit,
Not an auto was stirring, nor light bulb was lit,

1. Richard Nixon.

A hundred long stockings were hung on a pole,
In hopes that St. Nich'las would fill them with coal.
The children were nestled in front of the fire,
While a sign on the furnace read "This space for hire." . . .
I glanced out the window, and almost dropped dead,
When alongside eight reindeer attached to a sled,
I saw Santa, with flames in the seat of his britches,
Plop into a snowbank. His deer were in stitches. . . .
He laughed and he winked as he got down to work,
With a nature so gay as to drive Scrooge berserk.
Then gingerly patting the side that was sore,
He chuckled again and left via the door.
He huddled his team and addressed them, "Now, men,
Keep your eyes on the chimneys, they're working again!"
But I heard him exclaim, o'er the reindeers' hoorays,
"Happy Christmas to all: Welcome back, good old days!"

A Visit From Fred Astaire

by Judy Blumenthal

'Twas the night before Christmas, and all through the
	house,
The stereo was stirring up something by Strauss;
The boots were drip-drying on yesterday's *Times*,
And the rooms were all fragrant with aerosol limes,
The children were zipped up like soft gift-wrapped bundles
In Acrilan sleepers, in pine Workbench trundles,
When out on the terrace, 'twasn't hail, 'twasn't sleet . . .
'Twas the rat-a-tat tapping of two nimble feet.
As we both gazed astonished, the glass doors slid wide
And a slim urbane gentleman glided inside.

We could tell in a wink as he danced up the chair,
That our visitor could only be—Fred Astaire.
With a crisp boutonniere in his satin lapel,
He tapped up the staircase and tapped down as well.
He spoke not a word, but as light as a feather,
Laid out four pairs of tap shoes in new patent leather.
Then he whirled out the door (as we gathered our wits)
Singing, "Take off this Christmas and put on the Ritz!"

'Tis the End of October

by George Fairbanks

'Tis the end of October, and all through the store
Ev'ry clerk's in a frenzy across the main floor.
The time has arrived for the Yuletide display.
The manager told them that this was the day
To get out the Christmas tree, reindeer and sled.
The store is a fairyland—all green and red
And silvery bells can be seen up above.
It's the season for Santa Claus, food, cheer and love
So the manager hums as he goes out to see
If the windows are trimmed well and seasonably.
The one out in front shows St. Nick and his crew;
It's lavishly done: a spectacular view.
Another has Rudolph, and then one for tots
Shows Sesame Street ("Oh, they'll just love it lots").
The side of the store has a scene out of Dickens.
The manager beams and his pace sort of quickens
Till he comes to the last: a Nativity view;
For a moment he's puzzled, then gasps, "This is *who*?"

SIX

PARODIES FROM MAD MAGAZINE

Over the decades, *Mad* magazine has printed more parodies of well-known songs and poems than any other periodical. Most of them were written by Frank Jacobs, a former Manhattan writer now living in Burbank, California. Jacobs has contributed hundreds of pieces, both prose and verse, to *Mad*, much of it collected in a dozen or so paperbacks devoted exclusively to his work. I consider him a genius—the finest and funniest writer of humorous verse since Ogden Nash died in 1971. His four parodies of Moore's poem are reprinted here.

The Month Before Christmas

by Frank Jacobs

This first appeared in *Mad,* January 1969, and is reprinted in
*Mad Zaps the Human Race, and other horrors through the twisted
mind of Frank Jacobs,* a Mad Big Book, edited by Albert Feld-
stein (1984).

'Twas a month before Christmas, and all through the store
Each department was dripping with Yuletide decor;
The Muzak was blaring an out-of-tune carol
And fake snow was falling on "Ladies' Apparel."

I'd flown many miles from the North Pole this day
To check on reports which had caused me dismay;
I'd come to this store for but one special reason:
To see for myself what went on at this Season.

I hid in a corner and in a short while
I saw the Store President march down an aisle;
He shouted an order to "Turn the store tree on!"
And also the "NOEL" in blinding pink neon.

Up high, grandly hanging from twin gold supports,
Four hundred pink angels flew over "Men's Shorts;"
And towering over the Rear Mezzanine—
A 90-foot Day-Glo "Nativity Scene."

The clock on the wall said two minutes to nine;
The floorwalkers proudly all stood in a line;
I watched while the President smelled their carnations
Then called out his final command—"Man Your Stations!"

When out on the street there arose such a roar!
It rang to the rafters and boomed through the store!
It sounded exactly like street-repair drilling—
Or maybe another big Mafia killing!

I looked to the doors, and there banging the glass
Was a clamoring, shrieking, hysterical mass,
And I felt from the tone of each scream and each curse
That the "Spirit of Christmas" had changed for the worse.

The clock it struck nine and the door opened wide
And that great human avalanche thundered inside;
More fearsome than Sherman attacking Atlanta
Came parents and kiddies with just one goal—"Santa!"

In front stormed the mothers, all brandishing handbags
As heavy and deadly as 20-pound sandbags;
With gusto they swung them, the better to smash ears
Of innocent floorwalkers, buyers and cashiers.

Egged on by their parents, the kids had one aim:
To get to this man who was using my name;
They mobbed him and mauled him, the better to plead
For the presents they sought in their hour of greed.

The President watched with a gleam in his eye
As he thought of the toys that the parents would buy;
Of all Christmas come-ons, this crowd would attest
That a visit to "Santa" was clearly the best.

It all was too much for my soul to condone
And I let out a most unprofessional moan;
The crowd turned around, and I'll say for their sake
That they knew in an instant I wasn't a fake.

"I've had it," I told them, "with fast-buck promoting,
With gimmicks and come-ons and businessmen gloating;
This garish display of commercialized greed
Is so very UN-Christmas, it makes my heart bleed!"

The 1981 Night Before Christmas

by Frank Jacobs

This appeared in *Mad*, January 1981.

 'Twas the night before Christmas, and one thing was
    clear—
That old yuletide spirit no longer was here;
Inflation was rising; the crime rate was tripling;
The fuel bills were up, and our mortgage was crippling;

I opened a beer as I watched the TV,
Where Donny sang "O Holy Night" to Marie;[1]
The kids were in bed, getting sleep like they should;
Or else they were stoned, which was almost as good.

While ma with her ball-point was making a fuss
'Bout folks we'd sent cards to who'd sent none to us;
"Those ingrates," she thundered, and pounded her fist;
"Next year you can bet they'll be crossed off our list!"

When out in the yard came a deafening blare;
'Twas our burglar alarm, and I hollered, "Who's there?"
I turned on the searchlight, which lit up the night,
And, armed with my handgun, beheld a strange sight.

Some red-suited clown with a white beard immense
Was caught in our eight-foot electrified fence;
He called out, "I'm Santa! I bring you no malice!"
Said I, "If you're Santa, I'm Telly Savalas!"

But, lo, as his presence grew clearer to me,
I saw in the glare that it just might be he!

1. Donny and Marie Osmond, singing Mormon siblings who in 1981 had
their own television show.

I called off our doberman clawing his sleigh
And, frisking him twice, said, "I think he's okay."

I led him inside where he slumped in a chair,
And he poured out the following tale of despair;
"On Christmas eves past I was jolly and chuckling,
But now 'neath the pressures, I fear I am buckling.

"You'll note I've arrived with no reindeer this year,
And without them, my sleigh is much harder to steer;
Although I would like to continue to use them,
The wildlife officials believe I abuse them.

"To add to my problem, Ralph Nader dropped by
And told me my sleigh was unsafe in the sky;
I now must wear seatbelts, despite my objections,
And bring in the sleigh twice a year for inspections.

"Last April my workers came forth with demands,
And I soon had a general strike on my hands;
I couldn't afford to pay unionized elves,
So the missus and I did the work by ourselves.

"And then, later on, came additional trouble—
An avalanche left my fine workshop in rubble;
My Allstate insurance was worthless, because
They had shrewdly slipped in a 'no avalanche' clause.

"And after that came an I.R.S. audit;
The government claimed I was out to defraud it;
They finally nailed me for 65 grand,
Which I paid through the sale of my house and my land.

"And yet I persist, though it gives me a scare
Flying blind through the blanket of smog in the air;
Not to mention the hunters who fill me with dread,
Taking shots at my sleigh as I pass overhead.

"My torn-up red suit, and these bruises and swellings,
I got fighting muggers in multiple dwellings.
And if you should ask why I'm glowing tonight,
It's from flying too close to a nuclear site."

He rose from his chair and he heaved a great sigh,

And I couldn't help notice a tear in his eye;
"I've tried," he declared, "to reverse each defeat,
But I fear that today I've become obsolete."

He slumped out the door and returned to his sleigh,
And these last words he spoke as he went on his way;
"No longer can I do the job that's required;
If anyone asks, just say, 'Santa's retired!' "

The Night Before Christmas, 1999, or St. Nicholas Meets the Population Explosion

by Frank Jacobs

Reprinted from Frank Jacobs's paperback *Mad for Better or Verse,* edited by Albert Feldstein and illustrated by Paul Coker, Jr. (Signet Books, New American Library, 1968).

'Twas the night before Christmas,
  And all through the gloom
Not a creature was stirring;
  There just wasn't room;
The stockings were hanging
  In numbers so great,
We feared that the walls
  Would collapse from the weight!

The children like cattle
  Were packed off to bed;
We took a quick count;
  There were three-hundred head;
Not to mention the grown-ups—
  Those hundreds of dozens
Of uncles and inlaws
  And twice-removed cousins!

When outside the house
  There arose such a din!
I wanted to look
  But the mob held me in;
With pushing and shoving
  And cursing out loud,
In forty-five minutes
  I squeezed through the crowd!

Outside on the lawn
  I could see a fresh snow
Had covered the people
  Asleep down below;
And up in the sky
  What should strangely appear
But an overweight sleigh
  Pulled by countless reindeer!

They pulled and they tugged
  And they wheezed as they came,
And the red-suited driver
  Called each one by name:
"Now, Dasher! Now, Dancer!
  Now, Prancer and Vixen!
On, Comet! On, Cupid!
  On Donder and Blitzen!

"Now, Melvin! Now, Marvin!
  Now, Albert and Jasper!
On, Sidney! On, Seymour!
  On Harvey and Casper!

Now, Clifford! Now, Max"—
  But he stopped, far from through:
Our welcoming house-top
  Was coming in view!

Direct to our house-top
  The reindeer then sped
With the sleigh full of toys
  And St. Nick at the head;
And then like an earthquake
  I heard on the roof
The clomping and pounding
  Of each noisy hoof!

Before I could holler
  A warning of doom,
The whole aggregation
  Fell into the room;
And under a mountain
  Of plaster and brick
Mingled inlaws and reindeer
  And me and St. Nick;

He panted and sighed
  Like a man who was weary;
His shoulders were stooped
  And his outlook was dreary:
"I'm way behind schedule,"
  He said with a sigh,
"And I've been on the road
  Since the first of July!"

'Twas then that I noticed
    The great, monstrous sack,
Which he barely could hold
    On his poor, creaking back;
"Confound it!" he moaned,
    "Though my bag's full of toys,
I'm engulfed by the birthrate
    Of new girls and boys!"

Then, filling the stockings,
    He shook his sad face,
"This job is a killer!
    I can't take the pace!

This cluttered old world
    Is beyond my control!
There even are millions
    Up at the North Pole!

"Now I'm late!" he exclaimed,
    "And I really must hurry!
By now I should be
    Over Joplin, Missouri!"
But he managed to sigh
    As he drove out of sight,
"Happy Christmas to all,
    And to all a goodnight!"

If Moore's "The Night Before Christmas" Were Written by Robert W. Service

by Frank Jacobs

From the March 1968 issue of *Mad*.

A bunch of the boys were whooping it up
    on a Christmas Eve one year,
All full of cheap whiskey and hoping like hell
    that St. Nick would soon appear,

When right through the door and straight out of the night,
   which was icy and cold as a freezer,
Came a broken-down sled, pulled by eight mangy dogs,
   which were whipped by an old bearded geezer.

His teeth were half missing, and flapping his frame
   was a tatter of red-colored clothes;
He was covered with snow from his head to his toe,
   and an icicle hung from his nose;
The miners all cheered when the geezer appeared,
   and the poker game stopped in mid-bet;
Each sourdough smiled like a young, happy child
   at the thought of the gifts he would get.

They pushed him aside and went straight for his bag
   to be sure that they'd all get their share;
And, oh, how they cried when they found that inside
   there was nothing but old underwear;
So they plugged the old geezer, which was a great shame,
   for if anyone there had been sober,
He'd have known double-quick that it wasn't St. Nick,
   'cause it only was early October!

The Night Before Christmas
in "Hip Talk"

Mad published this in March 1959.

'Twas the night before Christmas, and all through the pad
Not a hipster was swinging, not even old Dad;

The chimney was draped in that stocking routine,
In hopes that "The Fat Man" would soon make the scene;

The wee cats were laid out all cool in their beds,
While sounds of the "Sugar Blues" wailed through their
    heads;
And my chick in her "Castro," and me on the floor,
Had just conked out cold for a forty-wink snore,

When out of left field there came on such a ribble,
I broke from my sack to see what was this dribble!
To the glasspane I cut like a B-Western movie,
Tuned in on the action, and, Man, was it groovy!

The moon and the snow were, like, faking together,
Which made the scene rock in the Day People weather,
When, what to these peepers should come on real queer
But a real crazy sleigh, and eight swinging reindeer,

With a hopped-up old driver on some frantic kick,
I was hip in a flash that it must be St. Nick.
Much faster than "Bird"[1] blew, this group was no drag,
And he rocked, and he rolled, and he pegged them by tag:

"Like, Dasher! Like, Dancer! Like, Prancer and Vixen!
Go, Comet! Go, Cupid! Go, Donder and Blitzen!
Fly over the shack! Make it over the pad!
Now cut out, Man! Cut out, Man! Cut out like mad!"

As sidemen in combos pick up as they stomp,
When they swing with the beat of a Dixieland Romp,
So up to the top of my bandstand they flew,
With the sleigh full of loot, and St. Nicholas, too.

And then, in a quick riff, I dug on the roof
The jumpin' and jivin' of each swinging hoof.
As I pulled in my noggin, and turned around fast,
Down the chimney came Nick like a hot trumpet blast.

He was wrapped up to kill, Man, a real kookie dresser!
And his rags were, like, way out! Pops! He was a gasser!

1. Charlie (Yardbird or Bird) Parker, alto saxophonist.

A sack full of goodies hung down to his tail,
And he looked like a postman with ''Basie's''[2] fan mail.

His lids—Man, they sizzled! His dimples were smiles!
His cheeks were like ''Dizzy's,''[3] his beak was like ''Miles' ''![4]
His puckered-up mouth was, like, blowing flat E,
And his chin hid behind a real crazy goatee!

The tip of a butt he had snagged in his choppers,
And he took a few drags just like all cool be-boppers;
He had a weird face, and a solid reet[5] middle
That bounced when he cracked, like a gutbucket fiddle!

He was shaking with meat, meaning he was no square,
And I flipped, 'cause I'd always thought he was ''longhair''!
But the glint in his eye and the beat in his touch
Soon gave me the message this cat was ''too much''!

He blew not a sound, but skipped right to his gig,
And stashed all the stockings, then came on real big,
And flashing a sign, like that old ''Schnozzle'' bit,
And playing it hip, up the chimney he split;

He flew to his skids, to his group blew a lick,
And they cut out real cool, on a wild frenzied kick.
But I heard him sound off, with a razz-a-ma-tazz:
"A cool Christmas to all, and, like, all of that jazz!"

2. Count Basie, pianist and orchestra leader.
3. Dizzy Gillespie, trumpeter.
4. Miles Davis, trumpeter.
5. Reet: good. From ''all reet'' meaning ''all right.''

SEVEN

SUBSTITUTE SANTAS

The Night Before Christmas: Revised Version

by Judy Carlson

This excellent parody appeared in *Seventeen* magazine, December 1981.

'Twas the night before Christmas, and I couldn't sleep.
My sister was snoring too loudly—the creep!
So I in my nightie, with socks on my feet,
Skipped out to the kitchen to see what was to eat.

I was stuffing down cookies when I heard someone humming
The theme song from *Star Wars*—someone was coming!
Then from our chimney, I heard a loud crash,
And out of the fireplace fell a girl (and some ash).

"Oh, hi," she said calmly, dripping snow water,
"I'm Holly St. Nicholas—Santa's granddaughter."
She was dressed in old jeans and had curly red hair,
And her coat that said "North Pole is Cool" had a tear.

"Where's Santa?" I asked. "I hope he's all right."
"Oh, yes," Holly said. "He's on TV tonight!
Johnny Carson asked Gramps to guest-host his show.
He needed exposure. He needed the dough.

His income from visiting stores wasn't good,
So he aquired an agent. He's gone Hollywood!
He's in *Christmas Lagoon*—co-starring Brooke Shields,
Next is *Smokey and Santa* with cute Sally Field."[1]

Then Holly Claus groaned as she looked in her sack.
"This bag is no feather—my poor aching back!"
"Some oranges and walnuts," I cried. "Is that *it*?"
She shrugged and said, "Yep. Inflation has hit."

Then she looked at her watch and said, "Oh, no! I'm late.
I must be in Oshkosh at twelve fifty-eight."
I looked at the reindeer. "Are these the well known?"
Holly said, "No—they have careers of their own.

"Comet and Cupid dance on Lawrence Welk.
Dasher's in nature films, passing off as an elk.
Fly! is a rock group with Prance, Dance, and Vixen.
Donder does nightclubs with impressions of Nixon.

"I've named these nice new ones after my favorite men!"
She sprang to her sleigh. "Time to call them again!
On Redford, Travolta, and B. Manilow!
On Pacino, De Niro, and John McEnroe![2]

"To the corner split-level, to the new shopping mall!
Dash away! Dash away! Dash away, all!"
Then I heard her exclaim as she lurched out of sight,
"Merry Christmas to all and to all a good night!"

1. Brooke Shields starred in *Blue Lagoon*, and Sally Field in *Smokey and the Bandit*.
2. For the benefit of readers a few decades hence, these are movie stars Robert Redford, John Travolta, Al Pacino, Robert De Niro; singer Barry Manilow; and former tennis champion John McEnroe.

A Visit From Jack Nicklaus

by Hugh A. Mulligan

This inspired parody about the golf champion Jack Nicklaus appeared in Hugh A. Mulligan's newspaper column "Mulligan's Stew," December 1982. Born in 1925, Mulligan has a Master's Degree in English literature from Harvard University, and has been a reporter and foreign correspondent for the Associated Press since 1951. He is the author of *No Place to Die: The Agony of Vietnam*, and other books on the human side of foreign affairs.

'Twas the night before Christmas, when all through the bar
Every golfer was stirring and guzzling a jar.
The lockers were loaded with lots of good cheer
In hopes that Jack Nicklaus soon would be here.

Our members had asked him to play for some charity,
And visions of birdies increased their hilarity.
The pro in his plus fours, and I in my cups,
Just ordered two more, and exclaimed "Bottom ups!"

When out on the ninth green arose such a racket,
I ran to the porch, but couldn't quite hack it.
A pair of old golf shoes that I didn't see
Sent me head over double knits near the first tee.

The galaxy of stars set loose in my brain
Gave a pale ghostly glow to familiar terrain.
And what should my bleary eyes see with a start
But eight dwarfish caddies and a golden golf cart.

At the wheel that blond chauffeur with great bearish paws,
I knew by his cardigan must be Nicklaus.
Much rarer than eagles, his helpers they came,
When Jack pulled a scorecard and called them by name.

Now Watson, now Weiskopf, now Palmer, Trevino!
On Stadler, on Crenshaw, on Snead and de Vicenzo![1]
As a nine iron,[2] hit crisply, will loft toward the pin,
Just miss the deep bunker and sometimes drop in,

So up to the clubhouse those caddies they flew
With that cart full of goodies and Nicklaus, too.
With the same fluid grace that turns effort to art,
The Golden Bear stepped from that elfin golf cart.

As our members and guests all gathered around,
Down the chimney Jack Nicklaus came with a bound.
He wore slacks of pastel, cerise or vermilion,
White shoes, yellow sweater—he looked like a million!

The Gucci golf bag that hung down from his back
Pronounced him a champion—no local hack.
His brow, he soon wrinkled as if reading a green,
His eyes, without twinkle, took in the whole scene.

A shy, modest smile spread over his face,
His "Aw, shucks, fellows!" grin, after scoring an ace.
The shoulders seemed broader than when on TV.
Why the name Golden Bear for this giant grizzly?

He was chubby, not plump, or what you'd call fat,
And the shock of blond hair bore a green Master's cap.
With a wink of his eye, Jack dug deep in his sack,
And handed out presents to bring our games back.

Like a huge sand remover and water hole freezer,
Making par golf so certain for any old geezer,
He spoke not a word but unbagged in a trice
A marvelous ointment to cure hook or slice.

Next a magical mashie with radar to the pin,

1. These are names of famous golfers: Tom Watson, Tom Weiskopf, Arnold
Palmer, Lee Trevino, Craig Stadler, Ben Crenshaw, Sam Snead, and Rob-
erto de Vicenzo.
2. The nine iron is a short-distance golf club for shots within a range of
110 yards. The club's face has a 47-degree angle to the perpendicular shaft
that enables it to loft a ball on a higher trajectory. "A silver wand curiously
warped at one end," was how John Updike once described it.

And a magnetized niblick[3] to help you chip in.
All this, and a putter that just couldn't miss,
And unloseable golf balls—what more could you wish?

Jack sprang to his cart, gave his caddies a holler,
And away they all flew like a taxpayer's dollar.
Those gifts vanished too, as moving to high gear,
He rattled my dreams with a loud parting Bronx cheer.

Now, Virginia, you see, I'm quite shattered because
Though I'm not sure of Santa, I know there's a Nicklaus!

A Visit From St. Nicholson

by Bob Rivers, Dennis Amero, and Brian Silva

This parody is recited on a 1987 album and audiotape produced by the Bob Rivers Comedy Corporation.

'Twas the fright before Christmas, no one up except me,
With a big bowl of popcorn, and watching TV.
I stretched, gave a yawn, settled back in my chair
In hopes that St. Nicholson soon would be there.
The children were lying awake without sleep.
They'd seen all his movies. He gives them the creeps.
I'd cued up *Cuckoo's Nest*,[1] with my trusty remote,

3. Niblick: a club used for jerking the ball out of sand or rough ground.
1. *One Flew Over the Cuckoo's Nest*, the movie in which Jack Nicholson
played a rapist confined to a mental institution.

To the part where he had all the nuts in the boat,
When out on the lawn there arose such a clatter
I turned off the set to see what was the matter.
And what to my wondering eyes should approach
But the Los Angeles Lakers, with Reiley,[2] their coach.
The limo was racing, the team at its heel,
And that's when I saw him, the man at the wheel.
He ranted and cursed, and flourished his swizzle stick.
I knew in a second it must be Jack Nick.
More rapid than Celtics, those Lakers they came.
Nick screamed like a mad man, and called them by name:
"Now Magic, now Worthy, now Scott and Kareem.
On Cooper, on Rambis, and the rest of the team."[3]
Down the chimney St. Nicholson came with a groan,
Then he brushed off the soot, and said, "Honey, I'm home."
He was wearing a trenchcoat, with beer it was stained,
And a shirt clawed to ribbons by Shirley MacLaine.[4]
He had a fat face and a flabby beer belly,
From too many trips to the bar and the deli.
"It's tough when an actor becomes fat and lazy.
I only get calls to play someone who's crazy,
Like a middle-aged has-been with washed-up career,
But I'll fix 'em all. I'll play Santa this year!"
So saying, he buried his head in the sack:
"Let's see what you get from your old buddy Jack.
A hatchet for daddy," he reared back his head,
"To scare all those buggers upstairs in their bed.
And a stiff drink for mommy inside a tall glass.
Something to kill all those bugs up her ass."
With a wink of his eye and a twist of his face,
He threw all the stockings into the fireplace.
What could I do? And what could I say?
What would I wear on my feet Christmas day?
I asked for a reason. Jack swiveled his head,
Looked me straight in the eyes, and here's what he said:

2. Pat Reiley.
3. Famous players on the Lakers basketball team.
4. A reference to love scenes involving Jack and Shirley in *Terms of Endearment*.

"Why? Do you wanna know why? Do you really wanna know why, pal? I'll tell you why. When you're out Christmas shopping, you know, doing your little Christmas things, with all your little Christmas friends, spreadin all that Christmas cheer, with those stupid Christmas songs, did ya ever think of pickin up a little something for old Jack, huh? Did ya ever stop to think what Jack might like for Christmas? You know, Jack, from the movies. Up on the big screen. Pouring his heart out, giving it everything he's got, day in and day out, just tryin as hard as he can to bring a tiny little bit of sunshine into your miserable little humdrum lives. Did ya ever think of good old Jack, huh? For a second? No! Not once! Maybe old Jack just wasn't that good, huh? Maybe I wasn't good enough in *The Postman Always Rings Twice*, actin my guts out for ya in that one. *Cuckoo's Nest! The Shining! Witches of* freakin *Eastwick! Prizzy's* freakin *Honor!*[5] All for you, pal! Just to brighten things up for ya. Not good enough, though, is it? No! You want me to brighten up the Christmas season too, huh? Isn't that what you want, pal? Okay, let's make things real bright around here. What do ya say we decorate the tree? String up these pretty lights here. Oh, she's lookin' brighter already. Why don't we take this cute little angel, and ram her on the top branch, huh? Huh? [laugh] How about some gasoline for the whole freakin thing. I mean, let's make her just as bright as she can be. What do ya say we light her up and chuck her through the old picture window here, huh, pal? No sense having a tree as bright as all that, not giving the neighbors a chance to see, don't ya think? Huh? There, aren't ya glad old Jack stopped by, huh? Huh? HUH?''

The flames towered bright in the cold wintry sky
As Nick made for his limo, and bade me good-bye.
And an age may unfold, ere I fail to regret
That visit from Nicholson—I'd sooner forget!
But I swear by the goosebumps all over my skin

5. Movies in which Nicholson played leading roles. More recently, he has been praised for his portrayal of the Joker in *Batman*.

I will always remember that devilish grin,
And his voice crying out, ere he faded from sight,
"Merry Christmas to all, and I hope I never see you again
    as long as I live, for cryin' out loud!"

A Visit From Sid Vicious

by Anonymous

Sid Vicious—his real name was John Simon Ritchie—was the bass guitarist with a British punk rock band called The Sex Pistols. Punk (or New Wave as it was known in England) was a British-concocted variety of hard rock, popular ten years ago before the punk burned out. It had a driving, incessant three-chord beat, and lyrics with four-letter words that stressed hate and violence toward everything associated with England's upper classes.

Punk audiences liked to spray each other and the performers with beer and spit, and to hurl bottles and obscene insults. The musicians would often respond in kind, and brawls were frequent. Both the musicians and their admirers flaunted carefully ripped clothes, slacks and capes made of garbage can liners, safety pins through their ears, noses and even cheeks, Nazi swastikas on leather jackets, dog collars around the neck, bizarre makeup, and crazy hair that was cropped, spiked, and dyed pink, blue, or green, sometimes two-toned.

In October 1979, Sid was arrested in New York City for the murder of his girl friend, go-go dancer Nancy Laura

Spungen, from Philadelphia. She was found stabbed to death in Sid's blood-spattered room at the Chelsea Hotel, near where Clement Moore lived and wrote his poem. Shortly after Sid's release on fifty-thousand-dollar bail, he tried to kill himself by slashing his wrists. Bail was revoked after he accosted the brother of punk singer Patti Smith, in a Manhattan bar, with a broken beer bottle. He was sent to Riker's Island for drug detoxification.

According to a lurid account in the *New York Times* (February 3, 1979), when Sid was released on his original bail he wore a T-shirt that said "I Love New York." His mother, who had dyed her hair red during Sid's sojourn at Rikers, accompanied him. Next morning, at 2 A.M., Sid was found dead of a heroin overdose at a party in Greenwich Village. Apparently he was too stupid to know, unless it was another suicide attempt, that his body could not tolerate the heroin doses to which he had become accustomed before he was detoxed. Hollywood made a forgettable movie about all this titled *Sid and Nancy*.

This parody appeared on Dana Richards's computer bulletin board in January 1990. If it was written, as I think it was, before Sid's arrest, the last five words are surely prophetic. Sid spent the Christmas of 1979 undergoing heroin withdrawal on Riker's Island.

'T was the night before New Years, when everyone's drunk,
Not a rocker was stirring, not even a punk.

The baggies[1] were hung by the phono with care,
In hopes that Saint Vicious, yes Sid, would be there.

The Ramones[2] were sold out, so we stayed in our sheds,
While visions of slammers still danced in our heads.

Suzie with hash pipe and I, dressed in black,
Had just settled down for a long-playing track.

1. Baggies: condoms.
2. The Ramones: British punk band.

When out in the alley there rose such a clatter,
I crawled from the couch to see what was the matter.

Away to the window I lurched with a crash,
Tearing a poster I'd had from the Clash.[3]

The strobe light, the acid, the new snorted snow,
Gave a luster of Day-Glo to objects below.

When what to my unfocussed eyes should appear,
But a miniature stage, and a band I could hear.

With a singer who danced; by the Pogo[4] he did.
I knew in an instant it must be Saint Sid.

More rapid than Springsteen,[5] their rhythm it came.
And he snarled, and he shouted, and called them by name:

"Now Strummer! Biafra! Now Joey Ramone!
On Bators! On Patti! On Cook and on Jones![6]

"To the top of the amps, kick over the wall!!!
Now ANARCHY, ANARCHY, ANARCHY ALL!!"[7]

As punks that before a big concert get high,
When they all start to Pogo, and mount to the sky,

So up to the window, the rockers they flew,
With powerful speakers, and Saint Vicious too.

And then in a twinkling I heard on the trunk,
The swearing and cursing of each famous punk.

3. The Clash: England's most famous punk rock group, less well known
in the United States.
4. The Pogo was a dance, sort of, in which one simply jumped up and
down as if on a pogo stick. During moments of ecstasy, entire audiences
of punk concerts would start to Pogo, hopping up and down, sometimes
falling over and injuring themselves.
5. Bruce Springsteen, a famous rock singer though not a punker.
6. Joe Strummer, guitarist for The Clash; Jello Biafra, singer for The Dead
Kennedys; Joey Ramone, singer for The Ramones; Stiv Bators, singer for
The Dead Boys; Patti Smith, punk vocalist and poet; Paul Cook, Sex Pistols'
drummer; Steve Jones, Sex Pistols' guitarist.
7. *Anarchy in the U.K.* was the Sex Pistols' first album, with Johnny Rotten
snarling the lyrics. The song is mentioned later in the poem.

As I drew on my pipe and was turning around,
Down the vent shaft, Saint Vicious, he came with a bound.

He was dressed all in black from his head to his foot,
And a chain on his shoulder was tarnished with soot,

A black leather jacket was flung on his back,
And he looked like a heretic freed from the rack.

His eyes, how they flashed, his smile, how merry!
He staggered right in, his breath smelled of sherry,

His darkly blue hair was drawn up in a spike,
And the rest of the punks were attired alike.

A portable mike he held tight in his hand,
"Holiday in the Sun" issued forth from the band.

To be followed by "Anarchy in the U.K.,"
"God Save the Queen," "EMI," and "My Way."[8]

The band played so loud, albums fell from my shelf,
And I gasped when I saw him in spite of myself.

A wink from his eye, and some dope for my head,
Soon gave me to know I should Pogo instead.

Then putting white powder inside of his nose,
And snorting it in, he said: "Damn all discos!"

He sprang to his stage, to the band gave a shout
And away they all jammed till Saint Vicious passed out.

But I heard him exclaim, with the last of his might,
"SCORCHING PUNK ROCK TO ALL, AND TOO AWFUL
    GOOD NIGHT!!!"

8. These are all notable punk songs. "God Save the Queen" called the
Queen a moron, and got The Sex Pistols banned from BBC programs.

A Farm Visit From St. Hick

by John Doyel

John Doyel, an inventor of toys and plastic gadgets, lives with his family in a landmarked house in the Chelsea district of Manhattan. The house, once owned by Clement Clarke Moore, is the oldest dwelling in Chelsea. In addition to a large and varied collection of Santa Clauses, Doyel collects and writes parodies of Moore's poem. This, his latest, was written shortly before Christmas 1989.

'Twas the night 'afore Christmas, when all through our
    house
Not a critter was stirrin', not even a mouse.
Red long johns were hung by the stove pipe with care,
In hopes that St. Hick, no less, soon would be there.
The chilen were scrunched up, all snug in their boggins,
While visions of Hershey bars danced in their noggins,
And ma with her flannels, and me with my booze,
Had just settled ourselves for a long winter snooze,
When out on the lawn there arose such a clatter,
I sprang from my bed to see what was the matter,
Away to the window I jumped in a dash,
Tore down the blind and threw up the sash.
The moon on the drifts of the fresh fallen snow
Gave the brightness of noontime to junk piled below.
Then into my view came the strangest of rigs,
A little ol' buggy and eight tiny pigs,
With a little old driver, so lively and quick,
I knew in a moment it must be St. Hick.
Faster than horses his piggies they came,
And he whistled and shouted and called them by name:
"Now Squealer! Now Oinker! Now Grunter and Snorker!
On, Fatso! On, Stupid! On, Hammy and Porker!

To the top of the porch, not down to the wallow.
No wigglin' and gruntin'—Go fly like a swallow!"
As clapboards before a fierce tornado scurry,
To crash into barns and fly up in a hurry,
So up to the housetop the piggies all flew
With the buggy of toys and St. Hick comin' too.
And then, by tarnation!, I heard on the roof
The scratchin' and pawin' of each piggy hoof.
As I pulled in my head and was turnin' around,
Down the stove pipe St. Hick, no less, came with a bound.
He was dressed in his work clothes, a boot on each foot,
And his Levis were messed up with ashes and soot.
A bundle of toys he had flung on his back,
And he looked like a hayseed just ope'nin' a sack.
His eyes how they watered! His look was so wary!
His cheeks were like cabbage, his nose was so scary.
A plug of Mail Pouch moved about in his cheeks,
And the beard on his chin had tobaccy-stained streaks.
And the stump of a pipe he held tight in his teeth,
And the smoke circled 'round his bald head like a wreath.
He had a broad bottom and a very fat belly
That shook when he laughed like a tub fulla jelly.
He was chunky and fat, a right scraggly old farmer,
But the sight of him standin' there made me feel warmer.
A wink of his eye and a twist of his bean
Soon let me to know that he wasn't too mean.
He didn't say nothin'—went straight to his work,
Filled our red union suits, and then turned with a jerk,
And pokin' his finger with a nosey intent,
And giving a nod up the stove pipe he went.
He sprang to his buggy, to his pigs gave a whistle,
And away they all zoomed like a hog stuck in thistle.
But I heard him a yellin', 'fore he drove outta sight,
"Git along, little piggies, I ain't got all night!"

Christmas in Cygnus

by Kay C Dee

This account of an extraterrestrial Santa visiting a space station on a colonized planet, presumably somewhere in the constellation of Cygnus (the Swan), was written in 1988 by Miss Dee when she was a freshman majoring in chemical and biomedical engineering at Carnegie Mellon University.

'Twas the night before Christmas and all through the galaxy
The home of each life form reached a state of normalaxy.

The stockings were Velcro-ed by Climate Control
In hopes that St. Nicholas would be on patrol.

The young ones had finally gotten to bed,
Their alarms set for five, and dreams in their heads.

The new coffee maker gave a soft gentle beep
As mama and I settled down for a sleep,

When outside the station there arose a loud roar!
I sprang from my bed and I ran out the door.

Away to the airlock yet faster I went,
Threw open the safety and looked out the vent.

The moon o'er the crest of Cygnus-13
Lit the night sky as brightly as I'd ever seen.

When on the horizon I happened to glance,
I saw Santa's rocket, five crafts in advance.

Three-quarters light speed, the rockets they came,
And through the receiver I heard all their names.

"Millennium Falcon, and Rama!"[1] he cried.
"Galileo, Apollo, Starship Enterprise!

1. The *Millennium Falcon* was a spaceship in the movie *Star Wars. Rama* is

"From earth to Andromeda, hit warp speed! Our flight
Must make stops at many a planet tonight!"

The deafening roar subsided at last
As each spaceship landed with a loud retroblast.

The glare from the flames made my vision quite dotty,
But I heard Santa say, "Now beam me in, Scotty."[2]

When my eyes had recovered, my jaw dropped down loose,
For Santa appeared to be from Betelgeuse![3]

His eyes, how they twinkled on the ends of their stalks!
His six arms swayed gently whenever he walked.

His skin was a beautiful dark shade of green.[4]
He'd the friendliest smile that I'd ever seen.

No mental telepathy passed 'twixt him and me.
He'd a job to complete, and places to be.

He filled all our stockings from a big bulging sack,
Saluted with one arm, and then was beamed back.

"Fire up the thrusters!" St. Nicholas said,
"But turn off your brights. I hear fog lies ahead."

His final transmission as they vanished from sight
Was "Merry Christmas to all, and to all a good night!"

---

a gigantic spacecraft featured in several science-fiction novels by Arthur
Clarke.
2. "Beam me in [or up or down], Scotty" are familiar orders given by
Captain Kirk, of *Starship Enterprise* (in the television and motion picture
series *Star Trek*), to his officer Scotty.
3. Betelgeuse is a "red giant" star about 500 million light years from earth,
and surrounded by a shell of matter four hundred times larger than our
entire solar system. It forms the right shoulder of the constellation Orion.
4. Miss Dee (the C, by the way, is not followed by a period because it is
her middle name, like the S in Harry S Truman) tells me that her parody
was inspired by a series of December covers of the science-fiction magazine
Galaxy. The covers of issues in the 1950s featured a green, multi-appen-
daged Santa Claus.

The Radio Santa's Night Before Christmas

by Harry Irving Phillips

Like Phillips's two previous parodies, this can be found in his book *On White or Rye* (Harper's, 1941).

'Twas the night before Christmas, when all through the
    house
Not a creature was stirring, not even a mouse;
The stockings were hung by the "speaker" with care,
For the program had said that St. Nick would be there;
The children were sleeplessly snuggled in bed,
Each hoping the batteries wouldn't go dead,
And mamma in her 'kerchief and I in my cap
Were just wishing a tenor would close his big trap,
When out of the radio came a great clatter
Of hoof beats and sleigh bells (but mostly the latter).
The jingle, the laughter and noise of the pack
Made me think that the ginger ale hour was back,
When what should my ears very presently hear
(Though the static was bad and the words not so clear)
But a voice saying "Kindly stand by, folks, because
The next voice you hear will be Joe Santa Claus,
Who is speaking tonight, we are happy to state,
O'er an unequaled hookup, extensive and great;
He will talk to more people from east coast to west
Than were talked to by Wendell and Frank at their best;[1]
This program will broadcast Yule greetings galore
To some seventy millions . . . and probably more."

1. Wendell Willkie, a Republican presidential candidate in 1940, and Franklin Roosevelt, his opponent.

Then next, to our joy, came a voice rather thick—
"Good evening! How are you, folks? This is Saint Nick!"
The patter of deers' feet then through the air came,
And he whistled and shouted and called them by name—
"Now Dasher! now, Dancer! now, Prancer and Vixen!
On, Comet! on, Cupid! on, Donder and Blitzen!—
These reindeer, dear folks, are the Superfine Brand,
Mild, Tender and Wholesome When Fresh or When Canned!

"To the top of the porch! To the top of the wall!
Now dash away! dash away! dash away all!—
This porch and the wall that we're using tonight
Is a Schmalz & Schmalz Product, the Builders Delight."

And then in a twinkle I heard on a roof
The pawing and prancing of each little hoof;
"This roof," said St. Nick, "is of copper, I think,
The product of National Roofers Corp., Inc."

As I tuned out the static I next heard him say,
"If you'll kindly stand by I'll a saxophone play."
Then he played lots of jazz with much gusto and swing,
Talked a while on the tariff—then started to sing!
He sang "Ridin' High" twice, and I don't need to say,
Like all radio songsters, "I'm King for a Day";
Next he pulled a few jokes, gave a short talk on sports,
And an organ recital and market reports.
His voice—how it pleased me, so rich and so merry—
Like Franklin's except it was deeper, oh, very;[2]
His laughter was that of a jolly old elf,
And I never did doubt it was Santa himself!
"I hope," he said gaily, "you people out there
Are pleased with this hour of mine on the air;
I now think I'll spring to my sleigh, folks, and when
I do it you'll know it's just quarter past ten!"

He sprang to his team, cracked his whip o'er his pets,
Saying, "All these eight reindeer smoke Blank cigarettes."
Then I heard him exclaim as he drove out of sight,
"Merry Christmas to all, and to all a good night—
By arrangement with Rosenberg, Plotz & Maloney—
The World-Famous Makers of Splendid Boloney!"

2. Joe Franklin, a well-known radio personality of the time.

EIGHT

PROVINCIAL AND SPECIALIZED PARODIES

Every year, as Christmas approaches, a number of parodies of Moore's poem are written to amuse members of various special groups: business firms, specialized professions, enthusiasts of a hobby, residents of a certain locale, members of a family, and so on. Many of them appear on Christmas cards. These take-offs vary from crude doggerel to clever verse, but in most cases are so saturated with names and terms unfamiliar to those outside the group, or with private jokes, that they have little interest outside their small circle of intended readers.

Two small books have been published that give Moore's original poem with brief commentary after most of the lines. Judith Viorst's *A Visit from St. Nicholas: To a Liberated Household*, illustrated by Norman Green, was published in 1977 by Simon and Schuster. (It had earlier appeared in *Redbook*, December 1976.) Viorst slightly altered some of the poem's lines to indicate that Santa is visiting Joyce, the feminist wife of Rich, and made a few other changes to indicate Joyce's feminist opinions. For example:

The moon on the chest of the new fallen snow . . .

The note for this line reads: "Actually, it's *breast* on the new fallen snow, but Joyce deplores this usage of breast, along with such sexist metaphors as Mother Nature, Father Time, and Manhattan."

In the line about Santa's "broad face," the word *broad* is changed to *wide,* followed by this note: "Actually, the face is described as *broad,* a word which in other contexts, Joyce observes, is exceedingly derogatory to women and ought, whenever possible, to be extirpated."

In 1989 Grosset and Dunlap published *Garfield's Night Before Christmas,* illustrated by Jim Davis, in which the comic-strip cat makes remarks about some of the lines, such as, "They look more like rain*dogs* to me," and, "I sure hope he knows how to drive that thing." When Santa comes down the chimney, Garfield says, "I prefer an elevator," and while the old gent is filling the stockings, Garfield cries, "More! More!" When Santa goes up the chimney, Garfield wonders, "How does he do that?" After the line "Tore open the shutters and threw up the sash," Garfield can think of nothing better to say than, "This had better be worth it."

A much funnier comment was made by writer Everett Bleiler's son, Richard, when he was a small child and the poem was read to him: "Why did he eat it?" he asked.

For those who collect parodies of Moore's poem, here is a partial list of specialized parodies not included in this collection.

"Campus Nosegay," by Marvin Miller, in *The Panacea,* an undergraduate journal of the Philadelphia College of Pharmacy and Science (December 1955).

"The Mucker's Dream," anonymous, in the *University of Arizona Bulletin—State Safety News,* January 1918. This parody about muckers (miners) opens: " 'Twas the night before Christmas, and all through the yard/ The branches were bare, and the ground frozen hard."

"A Visit from John L. Lewis," by Mrs. McDill McCown Gassman, in her book *Fragments* (Prairie City, Illinois: Decker

Press, 1948). It tells of a visit by John L. Lewis, the belligerent president of the United Mine Workers of America. " 'Twas the night before Christmas and all through the house/ Each creature was worried and felt like a louse."

"A Visit from St. Dick," by Judith Wax, a Chicago writer who died in an airplane crash in Chicago in 1979. This well-constructed parody, which ran in *Chicago* magazine (December 1975) swarms with the names of now forgotten Chicago politicians. St. Dick is the then Chicago mayor Richard Daley.

"De Night in De Front From Chreesmas," by Milt Gross (1895–1953), a popular humorist and cartoonist. This long parody, in the dialect of New York's Jewish community, was first published in the New York *World* in 1926. It was reprinted, with illustrations by Gross, as a small book (George H. Doran, 1927) that is now a rare collector's item.

"A Shaped-Up Santa," anonymous. This amusing parody depicts Santa as a well-muscled man, dedicated to physical fitness, who visits a similarly dedicated household. It was issued by Hallmark Greeting Cards as a booklet in 1979 (No. 175GBL 11–9). Hallmark refused reprint permission at any price and would not even disclose who wrote it.

"A Very Merry to Vivian and Arthur and Herman." Jean Harris, headmistress of the Madeira School in Washington, D.C., sent this parody as a Christmas card to three of her friends. Mrs. Harris is now in prison for the murder of Dr. Herman Tarnower in 1981. Her clever poem was read aloud to the court during her trial. It can be found in Diana Trilling's best-seller *Mrs. Harris: The Death of the Scarsdale Diet Doctor* (Harcourt Brace Jovanovich, 1981, pages 280–283).

"Santa Claus—Head Coach," anonymous. In 1990 Pro Set, a firm in Dallas, Texas, began issuing cards honoring football and hockey players. The new series opened with a card bearing a parody that begins:

'Twas the Night before Christmas and all through the land
The card biz was run like a lemonade stand.
While baseball and Topps had all the attention,
Football and hockey gained nary a mention.

There are surely hundreds of specialized parodies of

Moore's poem that I will never know about, and no doubt hundreds more will be written in the decades ahead. What follows are a few of special interest that can be understood and appreciated without extensive notes.

A Department Store Christmas

by Alice Jaynes

The *Ladies Home Journal* (December 1913) published this sad version of "Old Nick's" anger toward a salesgirl. Who, I wonder, was Ms. Jaynes?

'Twas the night before Christmas, when all in the shop,
Not a salesgirl nor wrapper but thought she would drop.

The cash children rushed with the money with care,[1]

With wan faces strained, hither, thither they fled,
While visions of reprimands flashed through each head,

At an hour when rich children were tied in nightcaps,
And settling themselves for their long winter naps.

From tables and counters arose such a clatter
Some terrible tragedy must be the matter.

The lights from the shining bulbs, white in their glow,
Gave luster of midday to objects below.

A salesgirl was selling small gifts. Like a flash
She tore open boxes and counted out cash,

1. The printers obviously lost a line here, ending with a rhyme for "care."

When what to my wondering ears should resound,
But a shrewish abuse you could hear aisles around,

From a woman, well gowned, who came just to kick,
I knew in a minute she was "the Old Nick."

She was dressed all in fur from her feet to her head,
And a comfortable feeling of opulence shed.

More rapid than reindeer, reproaches they came,
As she scolded and called the poor girl a harsh name.

"How stupid! You vixen! Don't dare answer back!
I'll report you at once for being so slack.

"My gifts never came. Now where can they be?
How such things can happen I really can't see!"

And giving a nod, up the store aisle she sailed,
Full of wrath that her own "Merry Christmas" had failed.

The salesgirl so pale went straight to her work,
For dozens of buyers forbade her to shirk.

More hours played the drama, long after she'd gone,
Delivery boys, women, cash girls struggled on.

In hundreds of stores, and in many a city,
This spells "Merry Christmas." Oh! good people, pity!

A Korean Christmas Carol

by Lieutenant Colonel Darrell T. Rathbun

I am indebted to Robert A. Baker, a retired professor of psychology, for sending me this parody. It first appeared in the Tokyo edition of the *Stars and Stripes*, October 22, 1951.

'Twas the night before Christmas, and all through the tent
Was the odor of fuel oil (the stove pipe was bent).
The shoe paks were hung by the oil stove with care;
In the hope that they'd issue each man a new pair.
The weary GI's were sacked-out in their beds,
And visions of sugar babies danced through their heads;
When up on the ridge line there rose such a clatter
(A Chinese machine gun had started to chatter),

I rushed to my rifle and threw back the bolt.
The rest of my tent-mates awoke with a jolt.
Outside we could hear our platoon sergeant Kelly,
A hard little man with a little pot belly.
"Come Yancey, come Clancey, come Connors and Watson,
Up Miller, up Shiller, up Baker and Dodson!"
We tumbled outside in a swirl of confusion,
So cold that each man could have used a transfusion.

"Get up on that hill-top and silence that Red,
And don't you come back till you're sure that he's dead."
Then putting his thumb up in front of his nose,
Sergeant Kelly took leave of us shivering Joes.
But we all heard him say in a voice soft and light:
"Merry Christmas to all—May you live through the night!"

Christmas Near the Moon

by Anonymous

On the day after Christmas 1968, the *New York Times* reported a Christmas day conversation between astronauts Frank Borman, James Lovell, and William Anders on the Apollo 8 mission, the world's first flight to the moon, and the Mission Control Center at the Manned Spacecraft Center in Houston. After Lovell wished the control team a Merry Christmas, the team responded: "We have some good words that originated at the Cape with a bunch of friends of yours, and it's sort of a paraphrase of a poem that you are probably familiar with. Do you read me Apollo 8?"

After an affirmative "You are loud and clear," someone on the team read the following anonymous parody:

'Twas the night before Christmas, and way out in space
The Apollo-8 crew had just won the moon race.
Their headsets were hung by the consoles with care
In hope that Chris Kraft[1] soon would be there.
Frank Borman was nestled all snug in his bed,
While visions of Refsmmat[2] danced in his head.
Jim Lovell on couch and Bill Anders in bay
Were racking their brains o'er a computer display,
When out of the DSKY[3] there 'rose such a clatter
Frank sprang from his bed to see what was the matter.
Away to the sextant he flew like a flash
To make sure the ship was not going to crash.

1. Christopher Columbus Kraft, Jr., a famous aerospace engineer who was then director of flight operations at the Houston Space Center.
2. Refsmmat: a display used to align navigation equipment.
3. DSKY: a computer's display and keyboard.

The light on the breast of the moon's jagged crust
Gave a luster of green cheese to gray lunar dust,
When what to his wondering eyes should appear
But a Burma Shave sign saying "Kilroy was here."[4]
But Frank was no fool, and he knew pretty quick
That they had been first. This was surely a trick!
More rapid than rockets his curses they came.
He turned to his crewmen and called them by name:
"Now Lovell, now Anders, please don't think I'd fall
For that old joke you've written up there on the wall."
They spoke not a word, but still grinning like elves
They laughed at their hoaxing in spite of themselves.
Frank sprang to his couch, to the ship gave a thrust,
And away they all flew past the gray lunar dust.
But we heard them exclaim ere they flew 'round the moon:
"Merry Christmas to Earth! We'll be back there real soon!"

Santa the Astronaut

by Anonymous

In the December 1963 issue of a periodical called *Press Breaks,*
this amusing parody was attributed to the staff of *Engineering
Outlook,* a bulletin published at the University of Illinois,
Urbana. Maybe someone can tell me who the Van Zant in
the parody is.

'Twas the night before Christmas, and all thru the plant,
Not a creature was working but me and Van Zant.

4. During World War II, and shortly before and after, it was a fad among
the military to scribble "Kilroy was here" on fences and the walls of
washrooms.

The specs were all written and ready to go,
In hopes that the drawings would soon be, also.
A batch had been finished, and already checked
But others were not, as you might well expect.
So we, both as zealous as Scrooge's poor clerk,
Had just settled ourselves for a long evening's work—
When out on the lawn there arose such a clatter,
We sprang from our desks to see what was the matter.
The security lights on the new-fallen snow
Gave the luster of blastoff to objects below.
When, what to our wondering eyes should appear,

But a miniature space capsule and eight tiny (but extremely
    powerful) hydrazine-propellant boosters tandem
    mounted in series so the pilot could steer;
And a little round astronaut, so lively and quick,
I thought for a moment he might be Saint Nick.
But then Van Zant asked me, "Did you hear him yell
All those names to his boosters as his capsule fell?
'Now Atlas! now Saturn, now Vanguard and Gemini!
Let's make our next landing beside that old Chiminey!
On Nike! on Redstone! on Titan and Polaris!
It's only tonight that Canaveral can spare us!' "
As we drew in our heads and were turning around,
Down the chimney the astronaut came with a bound.
He was dressed in a spacesuit from his head to his foot,
And his clothes were all tarnished with ashes and soot;
"This soot," he said, smiling, "is not from your chimney,
It's caused by the heat of atmospheric re-entry!"
A wink of his eye and a twist of his head
Soon put us at ease, although he then said:
"Tell me, are your schedules really so tight,
Or do you get overtime for working tonight?"
I looked at Van Zant; then he looked at me;
I said, "It's a matter of deadline, you see . . ."
"We've got a tough problem," Van Zant said with a groan,
"In hanging the micronite up in the T-zone."
The astronaut chuckled, "Well, that's why I'm here,
In packaging, I was the first engineer."

He spoke nothing more, but went straight to the work,
And studied the problem; then turned with a jerk,

He smilingly told us to take a good look,
And held out a Christmas tree ornament hook.
Even though we both knew he had found the solution,
By then we felt ripe for a state institution.
"Well, fellows," he said, "all your systems are go;
It looks A-OK, so I've now got to blow."
And laying a finger astride of his nose,
And giving a grin, up the chimney he rose.
He sprang to his capsule and into the door,
And then blasted off with a Titanesque roar.
"Happy Christmas," he yelled, as he flew out of sight,
"Keep your stuff simple and it's bound to be right!"

The Night Before the Morning After

by Gerald Weales

The *New Republic* published this political parody in its December 20, 1954, issue. Ike and Mamie are, of course, president Dwight Eisenhower and his wife. Harry is Harry Truman, and Joe is Joseph McCarthy, the Red-baiting Wisconsin senator. Other Republican political figures mentioned are then vice president Richard Nixon, presidential aide Sherman Adams, Secretary of State John Foster Dulles, and senators William Fife Knowland and Styles Bridges.

Gerald Weales is professor emeritus of English at the University of Pennsylvania, Philadelphia, and drama critic for *Commonweal*. He has written one novel, two children's books, and many books about American drama and its leading playwrights. His latest book, *Canned Goods as Caviar: American Film Comedy of the 1930s*, was published in 1985 by the University of Chicago Press.

'Twas the night before Christmas, an annual venture.
Not a creature was stirring, not even a censure.
The issues were hung undisturbed in the air
In the hope that no one would notice them there.
The Congress was nestled all snug in its bed,
While visions of '56 danced through its head.
Mamie in her kerchief and Ike in his cap
Had just settled in for a newspaperless nap,
When by Harry's back porch[1] there arose such hallooing,
Ike sprang from the bed to see what Joe was doing.
It took only one moment to set matters clear,
For out in Wisconsin they don't raise reindeer.
Ike sighed and he smiled, his fears were all laid;
It was only the gent from the Macy's parade,
Who reined in his deer, as if *he* controlled *them*,
As he sat in a chrome-plated sleigh from GM.
Then up leaped the deer from where they had been standing,
Came soft on the roof like the Columbine[2] landing.
He left them untethered for they were so tame
And quick as a contract, down the chimney he came.
He was a round little man, replete with affection,
As dear to Ike's heart as a landslide election.
He said not a word (or he wouldn't be quoted)
But opened the bag full of treasures he toted,
Began to unload all the rich Christmas rations,
Leaving first a kind word for the United Nations.
He offered to put between war and peace, distance,
By leaving the hope of, at least, coexistence.
He left dixon for Yates and a yates there for Dixon,[3]

1. Harry Truman added a back porch to the White House.
2. *Columbine* was the name of Ike's private plane.
3. The Dixon-Yates affair, as it was called, was one of Ike's greatest embarrassments. The Atomic Energy Commission had made plans for two private utilities, named Dixon and Yates after their presidents, to build a

And a new, plain cloth coat for Mrs. Dick Nixon.[4]
Some new clothes for Mamie, a golf ball for Dwight,
And then up the chimney he rose out of sight.
His take-off was swift from the White House high ridges,
On Adams! On Dulles! Soft Knowland! Soft Bridges!
And Ike heard him exclaim as he drove out of sight,
"Merry Christmas to all and to all a good-night."

---

steam plant in Memphis to supply that city with electric power. After the
contract was signed, it leaked out that Adolphe Wenzell, a government
consultant, who helped arrange the deal, was a vice president of the Boston
bank that had agreed to finance the new plant. Moreover, Ike's golfing
companion, Bobby Jones, was a director of the Yates firm. Ike denied all
conflicts of interest, but invoked executive privilege to hold back govern-
ment files. The affair blew over in 1955 when Memphis decided to build
its own power plant.
4. A reference to a line in Nixon's famous speech about his dog Checkers,
when he declared that he did not accept bribes and that his wife wore "a
plain cloth coat."

Rush to Passage
or The Night Before Recess

by Donald C. Morris

This more recent political parody was written in 1990 at my
request by a long-time friend, Don Morris, of Chevy Chase,
Maryland. We were classmates at the University of Chicago,
and later worked together in the university's press-relations
office. Don was editor of the school's humor magazine, the
Phoenix, then editor of the alumni magazine, and still later
managing editor of *Advertising Age*. "Rush to Passage" is

more closely and cleverly linked to the lines of Moore's poem than any other ballad in this book.

'Twas the night before recess, when all through the House
Not a solon was sleeping, not even a spouse;
The bills in the hopper were anxiously floating
In hopes that the congressmen soon would be voting.
The lobbyists waited, their dreams in suspense,
For visions of passage meant dollars and cents.
The President waited, his dog on his lap,
And had just settled down for a long winter's nap,
When in the rotunda arose such a noise,
The lobbyists jumped, like a bunch of schoolboys.
Away to the cloakroom they flew like a flash,
Unzipped their briefcases and readied their cash.
(There wasn't too much, so the congressmen learned,
For the Senate had taken its cut and adjourned.)
Then onto the scene, with back slaps and hellos,
Came the Speaker's stretch limo and some of his fellows.
And there, getting homage from every truth seeker,
Was their own peerless leader; it must be the Speaker.
More eager than ever, the Democrats came.
The Whip knew their leanings and called them by name:
"Now Rosty! now Aspin! now Pickle and Payne!
On Lantos! on Russo! on Brennan from Maine![1]

1. The House Democrats are Dan Rostenkowski, Les Aspin, J. J. "Jake" Pickle, Donald Payne, Tom Lantos, Martin Russo, and Joseph Brennan.

To the Capitol Dome from the end of the Mall,
Now dash away, dash away, dash away, all!"
As dry leaves that before the wild hurricane soar,
Representatives gather and mount to the floor.
Straight up to the chamber the congressmen fly,
Their thoughts on the goodies to come by and by.
As the tote machine stood by to tally the score—
The yea and the nay of each vote on the floor—
I sat up in my seat, and was turning around,
When up stood the Speaker. His gavel he found.
He wore a red tie and a natty blue suit
(He was dressed for a TV appearance, *sans doute*).
His mood was quite plain; he was certainly merry.
He looked like the cat that just ate the canary.
His eyes—how they twinkled. His colleagues were jolly;
Approaching adjournment, they chose not to dally.
The congressmen voted to pass every bill;
There was something for each, up on Capitol Hill.
The Speaker held veto-proof bills in his mitt;
"For opponents," he chortled, "I care not a whit."
He had a broad smile and a well-controlled belly,
That shook, when he laughed, like cold lox from the deli.
He loomed over the chamber; he looked like a bear.
(The minority leader was tearing his hair.)
A wink from the Speaker, a wave of his arm,
Soon gave us to know he intended no harm.
He spoke not a word—it was only December;
He'd fulfilled all the wishes of every member.
Then, laying his thumb to the tip of his nose
And giving a nod, from the dais he rose,
Headed down to his limo, gave a smile to his crew.
To his favorite restaurant, then, they all flew.
But I heard him exclaim, "If it's funding you lack,
Remember the season; put the arm on your PAC!"[2]

2. PAC: Political Action Committee, a fund-raising organization.

Santa Claus in Florida

by Anonymous

This parody, sent by Carolyn Fox, appeared in a Lake Worth, Florida, newspaper (name and date unknown) some time in 1971.

'Twas the night before Christmas and all through the town
No noses were frozen, no snow fluttered down.

No children in flannels were tucked into bed.
They all had on shorty pajamas instead.

To find wreaths of holly was not very hard,
For holly wreaths grew in each family's back yard.

In front of the houses were daddies and moms
Adorning the crotons and coconut palms.

The slumbering kiddies were dreaming with glee
That they would find water skis under the tree.

They knew that old Santa was well on his way
In a red Thunderbird instead of a sleigh.

He whizzed down the highways and zoomed up the roads
In a snappy convertible peddling his loads.

As he jumped from the car, he gave a deep chuckle.
He was dressed in Bermudas with an Ivy League buckle.

There weren't any chimneys, but that caused no gloom
For Santa came in through the Florida room.

He stopped at each house, staying only a minute,
While he emptied his bag of the toys that were in it.

Before he departed, he treated himself
To a glass of papaya juice left on the shelf.

He leaped in his car and put it in gear,
Then drove away whistling and singing with cheer.

We heard him exclaim as he went on his way,
"Good bye, sunny Florida—wish I could stay!"

Six Weeks Before Christmas
in Charlotte, North Carolina

by Ted Malone

Last year, while researching this book, I picked up a copy
of the 14th printing of *Ted Malone's Scrapbook* (Morrow, 1941).
When I got home and opened it, I found to my surprise that
a previous owner had pasted in the front of the book a parody
of Moore's poem. The parodist was none other than Malone
himself.

Elderly readers may recall Ted's popular radio program
"Between the Bookends," on which he read verse sent to
him by listeners. He was on the air every weekday from 1929
to 1944, when he left for London as a war correspondent for
the Blue Network. For years he was poetry editor of *Good
Housekeeping*.

The parody by Malone was clipped from an unidentified
Charlotte, North Carolina, newspaper, dated November 12,
1947. Above the poem are the following words: "Entertaining
feature of the speech by Ted Malone, nationally known radio
story-teller, at yesterday's Christmas Festival Luncheon, was
his version of 'Twas the Night Before Christmas.' Here it is:"

'Twas six weeks before Christmas, and all over Charlotte
Not a creature was stirring, not even a . . . mouse.[1]
The Merchants' Association said business was fair,
But hoped 'twould be better when Santa got there.

The merchants were all nestled snug in their beds,
While visions of Christmas rush danced in their heads.
Miss Jeffreys[2] in Hollywood and I in New York,
Had just settled down to our hard Autumn work,
When down North Carolina-way 'rose such a clatter,
Old Santa himself asked what was the matter.

Down from the north Pole he flew like a flash,
And landed in Mecklenburg County kershsmash!
The moon, had there been any new fallen snow,
Would have lustered like mid-day the objects below;
When what to his wandering eyes should appear,
But some eminent Charlottans with a bright new idea
Of starting off Christmas so lovely and quick
They could nick some new nickels for good old St. Nick,
And add to the holly and evergreens,
And of course to the mistletoe—beautiful queens!

Well, Santa, who naturally goes for such bounties,
Called on his reindeers and called on the counties:
"On Gaston! On Lincoln! On Cleveland! On Polk!
On Union! On Anson! On Richmond! On Hoke!"
In all directions he sent out his call
For the prettiest girls to be Queens of the Ball.

He drove Dasher and Dancer, Prancer and Vixen,
And his two Southern reindeers—Mason and Dixon.
Then gathering each girl in a brand new Ford sleigh,
He has brought all his queens here to slay us today.
Their eyes, how they twinkle! Their dimples, how merry!
Their cheeks are like roses—who said nose like a cherry?
Their droll little lips drawn up like a bow.

1. We don't know whether it was Ted Malone or the newspaper who
thought the word *harlot* here would offend the good people of Charlotte.
2. Anne Jeffreys, the movie star. She was born in Goldsboro, North Car-
olina.

That's enough of description, though there's more here
    below.
But what Santa did next everybody can see.
He lit Charlotte up like a huge Christmas tree.
The Merchants' Association helped hang the wreaths,
And the newspapers, too, and I should add to these
The radio stations strutted in with the canes,
But Old Santa himself provided the brains.

Miss Jeffreys and I, of course, heard of all this
And promptly decided it would not be amiss
If we came down today to join in the fun,
And maybe before everything was all done,
Anne could crown the Queen in a Christmas mood,
With a crown of holly from Hollywood.
I, chubby and plump, a right jolly old elf,
Whom some people laugh at in spite of themself,
Could play Santa Claus, and tell coast to coast
How Charlotte today is a host to a host
Of wonderful people, from nearby and far,
Who still believe in the Christmas star.

He's On His Way!

by Ray Linders

Here is another Florida tribute to Santa that I found in the
Haight Collection. Its date and source are not known, but it
probably appeared in a Florida newspaper. The author is
identified only as "Broward News Director."

It's the day before Christmas and easy to tell
That all of the kids are behaving quite well.

Why, even if they'd missed the earlier word
You know that by now they have certainly heard
That Santa, dear Santa's about to start out
With a toy-laden sleigh and a joy-laden shout.
They know, just as you do, what's going on now,
The elves at the North Pole are pushing the plow.
They're clearing a runway for reindeer to take
To the air when Old Santa releases the brake.
While Santa himself in his shop, in the back,
Is loading the year's crop of toys in a sack.
He's just about ready to take to the air,
With a tip of his hat and a nonchalant flair,
On his once-a-year trip to both hither and yon,
Seeking roofs of good children that he can land on.
Now here in South Florida youngsters despair
That he'll not make the scene in this tropical air,
With poinsettias flowering and hibiscus too,
Under skies that are warm and disgustingly blue.
Because everyone knows that a sleigh cannot land
In a snowless and blowless place covered with sand.
It's gritty and crunchy and rough on the blades,
And conditions are worser out close to the Glades
Where water's abundance is not very nice
When it hasn't the decency to turn into ice.
And even much worse than the lack of fine snow
Is the shortage of chimneys down which he can go
To chuckle and chortle, imagine how shocking,
As he tracks sand about when he's filling a stocking.
Well, kids, let me tell you it's silly to fall
In the trap of just fretting for nothing at all.
'Cause Santa's a whiz at untangling woes,
He just carries some snow in a snow-blowing hose.
He'll put it right down where he wants it to be,
And pull his red sleigh right straight up to your tree.
Take a tip from the Bonura kids, Jamie and John,[1]
That whatever your fears the big trip is still on.
Old Santa's about to take off on his flight
And despite all the problems, he'll be here tonight.

1. Can anyone tell me who the Bonura kids are?

'Twas the Night Before Christmas in the Desert

by Charlotte Van Bebber Cohen

Mrs. Cohen lives in Arizona with her husband, two children (whose creative musings led to her poem), and various pets. An abiding interest in literature, storytelling, and librarianship are, as she puts it, her "favorite irons in the fire." The poem was published as a picture book, colorfully illustrated by Mary Lou Ray Greer, in 1984.

'Twas the night before Christmas in the desert, you know.
Way out in the West where the tall cactus grow.

The stockings were hung near the wood-burning stove,
Where fragrant mesquite embers shimmered and glowed.

Such magical shadows were cast on the wall,
As Hank and Sal dozed to the crickets' soft call.

When all of a sudden there rose such a roar!
They sprang from their bunks and ran to the door!

What is it they wondered with eyes open wide. . . .
A bobcat or coyote with burrs in its hide?

The old timers say there are ghosts in the mountains . . .
Could it be old Geronimo whoopin' and hollerin'?

"Let's go back inside," said Sal with a shiver.
It was then that they spotted the long-awaited figure!

He had come in a pick-up all laden with toys,
And a list that he carried of good girls and boys!

He stood in the dry wash[1] all covered with dust,
Wearing Levis and boots, and a look you could trust.

And there right beside him—wonder of wonders—
Stood eight out-of-breath, but hardy roadrunners![2]

He looked at them fondly and called them by name,
That kindly old fellow of Santa Claus fame.

"Now Chula and Cholla, and Dusty and Streaker,
Pepita and Rita, and Chico and Treaker,
We've come many a mile through the star-spangled night,
And my little compañeros,[3] you've been such a delight!"

He set to work with a twinkling eye,
And he whistled a tune as he strolled right on by.

He filled up the stockings with wondrous toys,
With oranges, candy and more Christmas joys!

And then, just as quick as he'd come from the night,
He jumped into his pick-up and drove out of sight!

They heard his voice echoing from the foothills,
"MERRY CHRISTMAS, *amigos*!" Then the desert grew still.

1. Dry wash: the dry bed of a stream.
2. Roadrunner: a fast-running bird of the cuckoo family. It is the state bird
of New Mexico.
3. Compañeros: companions.

A Visit From St. Numismatist

by Dave Morice

This was written for a local coin collectors' club in Iowa City, and was published in their *Old Capitol Coin Club Newsletter*, December 1989. A numismatist is, of course, a coin collector and/or student of coins. Mr. Morice has kindly annotated it for me.

'Twas the night before Christmas, when all through the
    shop
Not a showcase was stirring, from bottom to top;
The slabs[1] were all hung by the proof sets[2] with care,
In hopes that St. Numismatist soon would be there;
The investors were nestled all snug in their beds,
While visions of portfolios danced in their heads;
And mamma with her checkbook, and I with my card,[3]
Had just settled ourselves to bid pretty hard,
When out on the bourse floor[4] there rose such a clatter,
I sprang from the auction to see what was the matter.
Away to the Red Book[5] I flew like a flash,
Tore open its pages, and counted my cash.
The Congress commemoratives[6] out on the snow
Had a lustrous, deep-mirror cameo.[7]

1. Slab: a plastic case made to encapsulate a professionally graded coin. The slab includes a certificate of authenticity.
2. Proof set: a set of coins, usually one of each denomination, struck from polished dies.
3. Card: credit card.
4. Bourse floor: the area at a coin show where dealers set up tables to display and sell their merchandise.
5. Red Book: the Bible of American numismatics; the most widely used guide to U.S. coins.
6. Congress commemoratives: gold five-dollar, silver dollar, and fifty-cent coins issued in 1989 to commemorate the bicentennial of the U.S. Congress.
7. Deep-mirror cameo: a highly reflective surface of a coin.

When what to my wondering eyepiece[8] appears
But a coin-covered sleigh, and eight telemarketeers,[9]
With a little old dealer, shaking his fist,
I knew that it must be St. Numismatist!
More rapid than Greysheets[10] his prices they came,
And he called out professional graders[11] by name:
"Now, Accugrade! now, PCGS! now, ANACS and NGC!
On, Hallmark! on, NCI! on, USGA and PNG![12]
To the full-step Jeffersons![13] To the split-band Mercs![14]
Now, grade away! Trade away all the fine works!"
As dollars that before the wild price-rises fly,
When they meet with an auctioneer, mount to the sky;
So up through the ceiling his bidders they flew,
With the sleigh, and all eight telemarketeers, too.
And then in a twinkling, I heard on the roof
A Three-Legged Buffalo[15] pawing each hoof.
As I pulled out my wallet, without any sound
St. Numismatist landed inside with a bound.
He was dressed all in coins, from his head to his foot,
And his clothes were all covered with gold-plated soot.
A bundle of plastic[16] he'd flung on his back,
Like a vest-pocket dealer[17] just opening his sack.

8. Eyepiece: a coin magnifying glass or jeweler's loop.

9. Telemarketeer: a dealer who sells coins by telephone.

10. Greysheet: a coin newsletter published mainly for dealers. It gives the weekly prices that coins realize at auctions.

11. Professional grader: a person who assigns condition grades to coins for a grading service company. The company then encapsulates the coin in a plastic slab along with a certificate and photograph of the coin as proof of authenticity.

12. The eight grading service companies listed in the poem are Accugrade (Accugrade Grading Service), PCGS (Professional Coin Grading Service), ANACS (American Numismatic Association Certificate Service), NGC (Numismatic Guaranty Corporation of America), Hallmark (Hallmark Grading Service), NCI (National Coin Investors, Inc.), USGA (United States Grading Association), PNG (Professional Numismatic Guild).

13. Jefferson: the Jefferson nickel, issued from 1938 to present.

14. Merc: the Mercury (or Winged Liberty) dime, issued from 1918 to 1945.

15. Three-Legged Buffalo: the 1937-D Buffalo (or Indian Head) nickel on which an error was made. The buffalo is missing one leg.

16. Plastic: the material that slabs are made of.

17. Vest-pocket dealer: a person who buys and sells coins at shows without

His dimes—how they twinkled!—his quarters how merry!
His cents were like gems, his halves like a cherry!
His dollar, an 1804[18]—you bet!—
Would cost twice as much as the national debt.
The Flying Eagle[19] held tight in his teeth
Was condition census,[20] from beak to its wreath.[21]
He had early coppers,[22] that metal-clad fella,
That shook when he laughed like a Coiled Hair Stella.[23]
He was wealthy and rich, a millionaire elf,
And I laughed at his ingots,[24] in spite of myself.
A twist of his head and a wink of his eye
Soon gave me to know there was nothing to buy;
He asked not a price, but went straight to his work,
And filled all my albums,[25] then turned with a jerk,
And held out to me another great gift:
A handsomely toned '55 Doubleshift.[26]
He sprang to his sleigh, and shouted some cheers,
And away he flew with his telemarketeers;
But I heard him exclaim, ere he priced out of sight,
"Hobby Christmas to all, and to all a good night!"

actually renting a table. "Vest-pocket" refers to the practice of carrying coins in a pocket-size coin wallet.

18. 1804 silver dollar: the "King of American Coins." In 1989 one sold at auction for $990,000.

19. Flying Eagle: the U.S. small cent officially issued in 1857 and 1858.

20. Condition census: the six highest graded coins for a given issue.

21. Beak to wreath: The Flying Eagle design depicts an eagle on the obverse and a wreath on the reverse.

22. Coppers: copper coins, especially those put out by the U.S. colonies.

23. Stella: the unofficial U.S. four-dollar goldpiece minted in 1879 and 1880. There are two varieties, "Coiled Hair" and "Flowing Hair," referring to the hairdo of "Miss Liberty," whose face appears on the obverse.

24. Ingots: gold bars, especially those issued in California by private companies or by the California State Assayer during the Gold Rush.

25. Album: a book made of thick cardboard with holes for inserting coins as they are obtained by year, mintmark, and/or variety.

26. '55 Doubleshift: the 1955 Lincoln cent error with a double image on the obverse.

The Night Before the Topology Final

by Kathleen E. (Kahila) Kustin

Ms. Kustin wrote this parody when she was a graduate student in mathematics at the University of Illinois, Urbana-Champaign. It won second prize in a poetry contest sponsored by the *Mathematical Intelligencer*, which printed it in Vol. 12, No. 1, 1990. I'll make no attempt to annotate it because notes would be unintelligible to nonmathematicians, whereas mathematicians should be able to appreciate the clever word play without help. Topology, let me add, studies the properties of objects that are unchanged when the object is given a continuous deformation, as if made of rubber.

'Twas the night before the Topology final
And all through the Haus (-dorff space)
Not a filter was stirring
Not even a filterbase.

An ϵ-net in a heap on the floor
I'm just too tired to work anymore!
The chapters all studied, all thoroughly read
And visions of Cantorsets dance in my head.

When out in my neighborhood there arose such a clatter
I ran to the window to see what was the matter
I stood and I stared, my amazement complete
'Twas the men from Topology, all most discrete
Cauchy and Moore and Tietze and Lindelöf
Zariski and Urysohn, Sorgenfrey, Tychonoff.

They came in a sleigh, and such was their fame
It was drawn by reindeer, and they called them by name
Now Metric, now Closure, now Inverse and Subbase
On Subnet, on Cover, on Product and Subspace.

And then in a twinkling they converged on my roof
(The reader must supply the proof!)
As I drew in my head and was turning around
Down the chimney they came with a *bound*.

They sat and discussed, till hours quite wee
Equivalent conditions for regularity
And whether it was an invariant fact
That a metric space is separable if it's compact
They showed me examples, and also a trick
Now, to what are $T_{3\,1/2}$ spaces homeomorphic?

It's quite late, and my fate is sealed
Under all this pressure, my brain has congealed!
But they meant no harm, it was quite unintentional
After all, they're only zero-dimensional.

So they sprang to their sleigh, urged a fast pace
And then they were gone, not leaving a trace
But I heard them exclaim, not at all formal
"Always remember, paracompact implies normal!"

A Visit From Saint Woz

by Marty Knight

I was not able to identify the author of this parody, taken
from Dana Richards's computer bulletin board and annotated
by his student, Ray Wagner. Saint Wozniac is Stephen (Steve)
Wozniac, a famous computer hacker who built the first Apple
computer in his garage.

'T was the night before Christmas, sounds all through the
    house,
the printer a'buzzing; the clicking of mouse.[1]

The floppies[2] were stored in their cases with care
in hopes that St. Wozniak soon would be there.

The children were nestled, all snug in their beds,
while TransWarp GS's[3] danced in their heads.

I need 3 megs more, but RAM costs a mint.[4]
I'm nodding off, waiting for my printer to print.

When out on the lawn there arose such a clatter,
I woke with a start, "Now what's the matter?"

Awakened from slumber I jumped up to see,
tripped over the dog and fell on my knee.

The moon shining onto the new fallen snow
formed a non-standard pallette with objects below.

When what to my poor bloodshot eyes should appear
but SHR graphics![5] Stereo sound do I hear!

With a sixteen bit chip[6] and new bug-free GSOS,[7]
I knew right away that it must be Saint Woz.

1. Mouse: a small device attached to a computer. By rolling it on the desk
top you can control the movement of the cursor on the display screen,
and move objects about on the screen.
2. Floppies are floppy disks—plastic disks on which information is stored.
3. TransWarp GS's: a highly souped-up modified Apple II GS Microcom-
puter. GS is an acronym for Graphics and Sound. The poem's main theme
is that Steve Wozniac, cofounder of Apple, will introduce Apple II GS +,
a newer, faster, better version.
4. A reference to the RAM shortage during the late 1980s. RAM stands
for Random-Access Memory. These are chips on which data can be tem-
porarily stored, to be wiped out when the computer is turned off, in
contrast to ROM (Read-Only Memory) chips which carry information built
permanently into the computer. "Three megs more" means that the nar-
rator needs three million more bits of RAM.
5. SHR graphics refers to a new system of faster and better displays.
6. A 16-bit chip is more powerful than the 8-bit chip used in the Apple II
computers.
7. GSOS: GS Operating System.

More rapid than TransWarp, his menus they came.
He clicked and he dragged and he called them by name.[8]

"Now Pulldowns, now Buttons, now Dialogs, too.[9]
On Finder, Mac Interface, we're faster than Mac II![10]

Blue slips for marketing! DTS better not scoff!
ProDOS[11] format for Technotes or I'll lay you all off!

You know lame excuses make customers sad;
well Macs in the schools make Applers mad."[12]

So up to the housetop his menus[13] they flew
with a sack full of RAM chips and Saint Wozniak, too.

I listened intently with my two little ears
to true stereo sound spreading holiday cheer.

As I was scratching my head and was turning around
down the chimney Saint Wozniak came with a bound.

He wore sneakers, a t-shirt, and faded blue jeans
stained with some soda (I think it was cream).

A bundle of chips he had slung on his back
and he looked like a hacker there searching his pack.

His eyes twinkled brightly, his dimples so merry,
his cheeks like twin apples, his nose like a cherry.

His droll little mouth smiled a smile O so grand,

8. The Apple mouse can be used to change the display by either a click operation or by dragging portions of the display to new positions on the screen. The display can also be changed by using the keyboard.
9. References to pulldown menus, on-screen buttons, and dialog boxes—all "user friendly" features of the Apple Macintosh.
10. A reference to other features of Macintosh II, at that time the top of the line.
11. ProDOS: Program Disk Operating System, a system used in the latter Apple IIe series.
12. This refers to the manufacturer's hope that Apple II would be widely used in elementary and high schools. However, the rival Macintosh line had features that made it more popular in the schools, to the chagrin of the Apple users.
13. Menus are options displayed on the screen, from which the user makes selections.

a full bearded chin, AppleLink[14] in his hand.

A thick slice of pizza he held with his teeth
while the steam from it circled his head like a wreath.

A plump little face and a round little belly;
he laughed and it shook like a bowl full of jelly.

He was chubby and plump; a right jolly old elf.
I laughed when I saw him—he resembled myself.

He winked his left eye and he twisted his head,
so I knew deep inside I had nothing to dread.

He said not a word, just went right to work.
He soldered and programmed,[15] then turned with a jerk.

Then placing his finger on top of that mess,
and giving a nod—POOF! fast GS!

He leaped to his ship as it rose from the ground,
up into the sky, and as he turned 'round

I heard him exclaim, ere he flew out of sight,
"GS plusses for all, and to all a good night!"

14. AppleLink is a network of Apple users that allows them to commu-
nicate with one another.
15. A tribute to Steve Wozniac's legendary skill in building and program-
ming computers.

A Computer's Night Before Christmas

by Anonymous

From the same bulletin board as the previous parody.

'Twas the night before Christmas, and all through the shop,
The computers were whirring; they never do stop.

The power was on and the temperature right,
In hopes that the input would feed back that night.

The system was ready, the program was coded,
And the memory drums had been carefully loaded.

While adding a holiday glow to the scene,
The lights on the console flashed blue, white, and green,

When out in the hall there arose such a clatter,
The programmer ran to see what was the matter.

Away to the hallway he flew like a flash,
Forgetting his key in his desperate dash.

He stood in the hallway and looked all about,
When the hall door slammed shut, and he was locked out.

Then in the computer room, what should appear,
But a miniature sleigh, and eight tiny reindeer.

And a little old man, who with scarcely a pause,
Chuckled "My name is Santa . . . but my log-in is Claus."

The computer was startled, confused by the name,
Then it buzzed as it heard the old fellow explain:

"This is Dasher and Dancer and Prancer and Vixen
And Comet and Cupid and Donder and Blitzen."

With all these odd names it was puzzled anew.
It hummed and it clanked, and a main circuit blew.

It searched in its memory core, trying to think,
Then the multi-line printer went out on the blink.

Unable to do its electronic job,
It said in a voice that was almost a sob:

"Your eyes how they twinkle, your dimples so merry,
Your cheeks so like roses, your nose like a cherry,

"Your smile, all these things I've been programmed to know,
And at data-recall I am more than so-so,

"But your name and address (we computers can't lie)
Are things that I just cannot identify.

"You've a jolly round face and a little round belly
That shakes when you laugh like a bowl full of jelly.

"My scanners can see you, but still I insist,
Since you're not in my program you cannot exist."

Old Santa just chuckled a merry "Ho-ho,"
And sat down to type out a quick word or so.

The keyboard clack-clattered, its sound sharp and clean,
As Nick entered this data into the machine:

"Kids everywhere know me, I come every year.
The presents I bring add to everyone's cheer.

"But you won't get a thing, that's as plain as can be.
Too bad your programmers forgot about me."

Then he faced the machine while he said with a shrug,
"Happy Christmas to all!", as he pulled out its plug.

The Worm Before Christmas

by Clement C. Morris

Clement C. Morris, an obvious play on Clement C. Moore, is the pseudonym for a group of five graduate students in the computer science department at the University of Illinois: David Bradley, Betty Cheng, Dan LaLiberte, Hal Render, and Greg Rogers. Written in 1988, the parody appeared on Dana Richards's computer bulletin board in January 1990.

 I will not try to explain all the computer terms, some of which are already dated, but some comments on "worm" will be essential to understanding the ballad. A *worm* is an unauthorized computer program that can shut down a system by "eating" portions of its memory, or clogging it with useless information. A *virus*, mentioned in the last stanza, is a small piece of computer code that hides inside legitimate programs until something triggers it, at which point it reproduces and sends copies of itself through a network to other machines. Like an epidemic it can infect thousands of computers, destroying valuable data and wasting enormous staff time in getting rid of it. Programs designed to detect and stop viruses are called *vaccines*. Other kinds of computer sabotage are called *time bombs*, *logic bombs*, and *Trojan horses*.

There really was a Morris's worm. In 1988 Robert Tappan Morris, then a Cornell University graduate student, tapped his malignant worm into a computer network and crippled some six thousand computers. He was sentenced in 1990, fined ten thousand dollars, and given three years' probation. It was the nation's first sentence for this type of computer crime.

'Twas the night before finals, and all through the lab
Not a student was sleeping, not even McNabb.[1]

1. When this ballad appeared on Dana Richards's bulletin board, the authors added: "We would like to apologize to Dave McNabb [another com-

Their projects were finished, completed with care,
In hopes that the grades would be easy (and fair).

The students were wired with caffeine in their veins,
While visions of quals nearly drove them insane.
With piles of books and a brand new highlighter,
I had just settled down for another all nighter—

When out from our gateways arose such a clatter,
I sprang from my desk to see what was the matter;
Away to the console I flew like a flash,
And logged in as root to fend off a crash.

The windows displayed on my brand new Sun-3,
Gave oodles of info—some in 3-D.
When, what to my burning red eyes should appear
But dozens of "nobody" jobs. Oh dear!

With a blitzkrieg invasion, so virulent and firm,
I knew in a moment, 'twas Morris's Worm!
More rapid than eagles his processes came,
And they forked and exec'ed and they copied by name:

"Now Dasher! Now Dancer! Now, Prancer and Vixen!
On Comet! On Cupid! On Donder and Blitzen!
To the sites in .rhosts and host.equiv[2]
Now, dash away! dash away! dash away all!"

And then in a twinkling, I heard on the phone,
The complaints of the users. (Thought I was alone!)

---

puter science student at the University of Illinois] for any detrimental
references to his sleeping habits or lack thereof. Unfortunately, we couldn't
think of anything else that rhymes with 'lab.' "
2. To be read: "dot are-hosts and hosts dot equiv." I am told that these
are system files containing lists of computer names. The line scans, but I
see no way to make it rhyme with the next line. The authors comment on
this stanza as follows:

> The machines dasher.cs.uiuc.edu, dancer.cs.uiuc.ed, prancer.cs.uiuc.
> edu, etc. have been renamed deer1, deer2, deer3, etc. so as not to
> confuse the already burdened students who use those machines. We
> regret that this poem reflects the older naming scheme and hope it
> does not confuse the network administrator at your site.

"The load is too high!" and "I can't read my files!"
"I can't send my mail over miles and miles!"

I unplugged the net, and was turning around,
When the worm-ridden system went down with a bound.
I fretted. I frittered. I sweated. I wept.
Then finally I core dumped the worm in /tmp.[3]

It was smart and pervasive, a right jolly old stealth,
And I laughed when I saw it, in spite of myself.
A look at the dump of that invasive thread
Soon gave me to know we had nothing to dread.

The next day was slow with no network connections,
For we wanted no more of those pesky infections.
But in spite of the news and the noise and the clatter,
Soon all became normal, as if naught were the matter.

Then later that month while we all were away,
A virus came calling and then went away.
The system then told us, when we logged in one night:
"Happy Christmas to all! (You guys ain't so bright.)"

Holmes and Watson Have a Visitor

by William E. Dunning

Bill Dunning is an English instructor and program director at KSFR, a local public radio station at Santa Fe Community College, in Santa Fe, New Mexico, and a freelance writer, principally of music reviews. Along with John Shaw (see note 10 below) and others, he is a founding member of The Broth-

3. To be read: "slash temp."

ers Three of Moriarty, a group of Sherlock Holmes fans in the area. His parody appeared in the *Baker Street Journal*, Volume 25, December 1975.

'Twas the night before Christmas at 2-2-1-B.[1]
Not a creature was stirring—not even me.
Holmes was relaxing, his tie and his collar loose.
We two had just eaten old Baker's black-barred goose,[2]
And were watching the logs in the soldered grate[3] glow,
When Holmes rang Mrs. Hudson, seventeen steps below.[4]
"Some eggnog, Mrs. Hudson, if you wouldn't mind,
With, my dear lady, if you'd be so kind,
Plenty of Scotch and just seven-percent egg."[5]
When she left, Sherlock stared at his cap on its peg.
Soon the woman returned with our holiday toast,
Along with a bowl of some chestnuts to roast.
When Holmes twitched his ears like a hound on the scent,
I saw through the bow window a curious gent.

"Well, Watson, just what d'you make of that bloke?"
I peered through the mixture of fog, snow, and smoke.
"He is portly, of course, and he wears a full beard,
And—I say, Holmes—that red suit is weird!"

"Tut, tut," my friend clucked, with a sardonic smile,
"You make up in bluntness your wanting of style.
Observe his knees, Watson, all covered with soot,

1. 221B was, of course, where Holmes and Watson shared a second-floor apartment.
2. Henry Baker's Christmas goose plays a major role in "The Adventure of the Blue Carbuncle." It is described as "white, with a black bar across the tail."
3. In the same story mentioned above there is a reference to the loose bar of a grate that had been repaired by soldering. We learn here that Holmes's grate had been similarly repaired.
4. Mrs. Hudson was Holmes's landlady. She lived on the first floor, reached from Holmes's floor by a stairway of seventeen steps.
5. During his early years, when Holmes was addicted to cocaine, he preferred to inject himself with a seven-percent solution of the drug.

And a flake of roof-slate that still clings to one boot.
His beard is the cut of an old-fashioned Dutchman.[6]
By simply observing, you can surely learn much, man.
The fur of his coat-trim, I beg you to note,
Is the style of the Eskimo—keeps him afloat
In case he should happen to fall in the water.
Perspiring in snowfall? Our climate is hotter
Than what he is used to, that fact is quite plain.
You observe, my good doctor, yet don't use your brain."

"But dash it all, Holmes," I replied in a fuss,
"I think that the fellow comes to see us!"
"Elementary! Watson, my dear foil and friend,
Notice the pattern his searching steps wend."
Mrs. Hudson withdrew then to answer the door.
Holmes mused to himself, "But what on earth for?
Why would that gentleman come to see me?
What case could I solve for a chap such as he?"

My eyes opened wide when the visitor entered.
A game seemed afoot. My hooks were all tentered!
"Good evening," said Holmes, "and the best of the season!
Your visit is welcome, but what is the reason?
You've come a long way from the distant North Pole."
[Holmes, you are amazing! Upon my soul!]
"From the smell of your pipe, I deduce that's your home.
Your brand of tobacco's sold only in Nome.
And the compass that hangs from your wide leather belt
Shows S in all four directions. The pelt
On the trim of your coat, sir, I venture to say,
Is native to Greenland, or old Hudson's Bay.
But sit yourself down, and pray tell us your case,
For I know that, tonight, you really must race."

"Quite true," said the visitor. "Soon I must go,
And may I assume that my name you now know?"
Holmes nodded, then wrote on a small piece of paper
The name of the man who had brought us this caper.
When he showed him the note, the visitor nodded,

6. The Dutch-cut beard implies the Dutch origin of Santa Claus among
the Dutch settlers of Manhattan.

Then Holmes, with a grin, the note tightly wadded
And threw it across the room into the fire.[7]
[He does things like that just to increase my ire!]
"Perhaps you bring me a case of identity,
For you have a number of names. It's insanity
To know how you're called in various lands."
"Not at all," said the visitor, resting his hands
On the shoulders of Sherlock. "I hear of you oft."
[The phrase was familiar. Could the man be Mycroft?[8]
A certain resemblance, yes, at the waist—
But no, let me judge not the fellow in haste!]
"I come to you, yes, but not with a mystery.
You know who I am so you must know my history."

Holmes's grey eyes grew dim, and curiously hot,
An emotion not seen since the time I was shot.[9]
"Yes, Sherlock, my boy, I have brought you a present,
A little, ah, something to make your life pleasant."
So saying, he lifted the coat from his middle
And produced to our gaze a marvelous fiddle.
Holmes was left speechless, and staring with awe,
'Til finally he managed the one word, "Pshaw!"[10]
The visitor chuckled. "I look like him slightly,
As well as your brother." His eyes twinkled brightly.
"I really don't know," sputtered Holmes, "how to thank you.
You know the esteem in which we all rank you."

Holmes took and examined the musical gift.
"Play it now," said our guest. "Give your spirits a lift!"

7. In "The Adventure of the Cardboard Box," Holmes refused to name a
criminal in the presence of Watson. Instead, he scribbled the man's name
on the back of his visiting card "and threw it over to Lestrade."
8. Holmes's older brother, Mycroft, had a massive girth that resembled
the girth of Santa Claus. "I hear of Sherlock everywhere," Mycroft said
to Watson (in "The Greek Interpreter"), "since you became his chronicler."
9. One of Holmes's rare expressions of emotion occurred when Watson
was superficially wounded by a bullet in "The Adventure of the Three
Garidebs." "You are not hurt, Watson? For God's sake, say you are not
hurt!"
10. Pshaw!: a subtle pun on the name of John Bennett Shaw, a famous
Sherlockian scholar and collector who, if he had a white beard, would
resemble Santa Claus.

"Observe, Watson," said Holmes, "this small label inside.
Stradivarius, it says, if my eyes are a guide!"

The visitor, seeing my friend was uneasy,
Stood up to leave, with a brisk manner breezy.
"I must be getting along now, my boys.
Lots of dolls to deliver, and candy, and toys!"
Then turning to me as I sat there so lambish,
He said, "No, I haven't forgotten you, Hamish![11]
Here's a new set of pens and a barrel of 'Ship's' "[12]
He laughed as he stood with his hands on his hips.
Producing the gifts from an inside coat pocket,
He turned to the door and began to unlock it.

"But wait, sir!" cried Holmes. "Won't you leave by the chim-
    ney,
As you usually do from Land's End to Bimini?
Your vast reputation, from Rome to the Isthmus,
Is climbing down everyone's chimney at Christmas."
"All right, I will, then, but please do me a favor.
Remove that jackknife,[13] for I fear it might waver,
And catch on my coat, perhaps even tear it.
In this cold freezing weather I surely must wear it."
Holmes took from the mantel his knife, and his letters
From innocent widows and impoverished debtors.
Our visitor laid by his nose a short finger,
And rose up the flue—refusing to linger.

"Now, Watson," said Holmes, "you must never reveal
That what you have witnessed tonight here was real.

11. In "The Man With the Twisted Lip," Mrs. Watson, for an unaccountable
reason that has been much debated, calls her husband James. We know
that John Watson's middle initial was H. It has been conjectured that the
H stood for Hamish, the Gaelic form of James. Watson's wife may have
liked to call him James, but as a child his parents probably called him
Hamish, the name Santa Claus would remember.
12. Ship's: British slang for "Schippers Tabak Special," a blend of strong
tobacco imported from Holland. When Holmes and Watson first met and
decided to share rooms, Holmes asked: "You don't mind the smell of
strong tobacco, I hope?" Watson replied: "I always smoke 'Ship's' myself."
13. Holmes kept his unanswered letters pinned with a large pocketknife
to the center of his wooden mantelpiece.

Just think of the damage to my reputation.
Putting emotion before ratiocination.
Tell the story, instead, in the following mode:
Say I purchased the fiddle on Tottenham Road[14]
From a peddler or pawnbroker. I am quite sure
You can give it some plausible dressing with your
Writing skill. Of course you now know who our visitor was."
"Yes, his name is Kris Kringle, also Santa Claus,
Saint Nick, Father Christmas, or maybe Befana—
Disguised as an elderly woman or nanna."
Mused Holmes, "I think he could teach me that trick
If only he'd not left our lodgings so quick."

Holmes rested the fiddle sideways on his knee
And started to play it to entertain me.
He paused when halfway through the song "Deck the Hall,"
And we heard from the roof, "Happy Christmas to all!"
As our visitor's reindeer took off on their flight,
"To all your Irregulars,[15] a pleasant good night!"

14. Watson followed Holmes's advice: In "The Adventure of the Cardboard
Box" he gave a false account of how his friend acquired his Stradivarius:
"We had a pleasant little meal together, during which Holmes would talk
of nothing but violins, narrating with great exultation how he had pur-
chased his Stradivarius which was worth at least five hundred guineas,
at a Jew broker's in Tottenham Court Road for fifty-five shillings."
15. The Baker Street Irregulars, an organization dedicated to the study of
Watson's narratives, is named after a group of street Arabs in London that
Holmes recruited to assist him in obtaining information.

The Spirit of Fire

by Anonymous

Carolyn Fox sent me this parody. It appeared in *White Caps*, December 10, 1963, a newsletter published for employees of the White Cap Company, a division of Continental Can, in Chicago.

'Twas the night before Christmas, and all through the house
Not a creature was stirring, not even a mouse,
When down through the chimney all covered with soot,
Came the "Spirit of Fire"—an ugly galoot.
His eyes glowed like embers, his features were stern,
As he looked all around for something to burn.
What he saw made him grumble, his anger grew higher,
For there wasn't a thing that would start a good fire.
No door had been blocked by the big Christmas tree;
It stood in the corner leaving passageways free.
The lights that glowed brightly for Betty and Tim
Had been hung with precaution so none touched a limb.
All wiring was new, not a break could be seen,
And wet sand at its base kept the tree nice and green.
The tree had been trimmed by a mother insistent
That the ornaments used be fire resistant.
And mother had known all the things to avoid,
Like cotton and paper, and plain celluloid.
Rock wool, metal icicles, trinkets of glass
Gave life to the tree; it really had class.
And would you believe it, right next to the tree
Was a suitable box for holding debris!
A place to throw wrappings of paper and string
From all of the gifts that Santa might bring.
The ugly galoot was so mad he could bust,
As he climbed up the chimney in utter disgust,

For the folks in this home had paid close attention,
To all of the rules of good "Fire Prevention."

The Night Before Thanksgiving
or "Owed" to Lee Iacocca

by Eliot Pfanstiehl

Mr. Pfanstiehl is the executive director of the Strathmore Hall Arts Center in Montgomery County, Maryland. He wrote his parody in 1987 to document what happened when he, his wife, and his two children drove their 1986 Dodge Caravan from Washington to Chicago and back over Thanksgiving for a family reunion.

The ballad was addressed and sent to Lee Iacocca, chairman of the Chrysler Corporation. Eliot tells me he received only a form letter from Chrysler directing him to read the small print in his warranty.

'Twas the night 'fore Thanksgiving and all through the house,
Not a child was stirring, just me and my spouse.

Our car was full-packed so that just before noon,
We'd be off to our 18-year family re-u-oon.

I drove the first shift, while Mama with her map,
Plotted routes from D.C. to Chicago and back.

When under the hood there arose such a clatter,
I sprang to attention, "Hey, what is the matter?"

While cruising at 60 near Cleveland, Ohio,
I felt something slipping, "Oh me!" then, "Oh My! No!"

The hill we were climbing was one of the lower,
Were we going fast? Nope, we're going much slower!

When what to our wondering eyes should appear,
But our car—going nowhere—although 'twas in gear.

With a little more testing of engine and such,
I knew in a flash that we'd lost our whole clutch.

More rapid than eagles, our speed now descending,
I muttered some words you'd find clearly offending.

"Perhaps with a Honda, or Chevy or Olds,
But NOT with a Chrysler! ('cause your word is Gold!)"

Since we're only 2 years on our 5/50 Plan,
Then our powertrain's covered . . . or so said the man.

Hey, we're gonna be late, but they'll fix up our van,
And they'll send that big bill to Detroit . . . to your man.

So, first came the tow truck who found a Dodge shop,
We were lucky to find them, they put the car up.

And then, in a twinkling, the guy says to me,
"Your *manual* transmission's not covered, I see . . ."

As I sucked in my breath and was coming around,
He added ". . . and no parts that fit can be found!"

Though he'd called other shops, seems he simply can't find,
Replacement clutch plates for a Dodge in a bind.

"If you leave the car here, we can fix it by Friday.
Cost 500 bucks (plus the tow) . . . happy holiday!"

My jaw how it grimaced, my pulse how it quickened.
We couldn't afford this, my stomach was sickened.

My dry little mouth was drawn tight with despair,
"There's something quite wrong here, this just isn't fair."

For a clutch to wear out in just over two years
Isn't normal, you know, there's a *defect* I fear.

It isn't my foot, my Toyota's old clutch
Took some 85,000 to wear down this much.

No, I really believe that the flaw's in design,
It's too heavy a van for a clutch such as mine.

See this clutch is "lightweight," and they don't make an-
        other,
Chrysler says, "It's not worth it, too few of 'em, brother."

The rental car ate, of our savings, the rest,
And I spoke not a word, but drove 8 hours west.

Now we're finally at home, and the bill's coming due,
I am stuck with a debt I can't pay (. . . how 'bout you?)

And it burns me no end I paid all of that dough,
For a spanking new car 2 years later won't go.

So my new clutch will last, only 2 years or 3,
While I'm driving a lemon, well, you're off scott free.

Still, I heard you exclaim on t.v. just last night,
"When *we* sell you a car, *you can bet it's made right!*"

NINE

PARODIES IN DIALECT

The Night Before Chanukah

by Anonymous

Several friends provided versions of this Yiddish parody. It goes back at least twenty-five years, but I was unable to uncover its origin. Most Yiddish words have a variety of spellings, and no two versions of the poem, among those sent to me, are alike in spellings. The footnotes should, in any case, make the meaning of the poem clear.

I have not included a much longer parody, in the dialect of New York City's Jewish immigrants, that was written by Milt Gross, one of the nation's most popular humorists and cartoonists. Titled "De Night in de Front from Chreesmas," it first ran in the New York *World* in 1926. A reprinting in book form the following year, with illustrations by the author, is now a rare collector's item.

'T was the night before Chanukah,[1] *boichecks* and *maidels*,[2]
Not a sound could be heard, not even the *draidels*.[3]

The *Menorah*[4] was set by the chimney, alight.
In the kitchen the *Bubbie*[5] was choppin' a bite.

Salami, pastrami, a *glassele tay*,[6]
And *zoyereh*[7] pickles with bagels—*Oi vei!*[8]

Gesundt[9] and *geschmack*[10] the *kinderlach*[11] felt,
While dreaming of *taiglach*[12] and Chanukah *gelt*.[13]

The alarm clock was sitting, a *kluppen* and *ticken*,[14]
And Bubbie was carving a *shtickele*[15] chicken.

A *tummel*[16] arose like a thousand *beruches*.[17]
Santa had fallen and broken his *tuchis*.[18]

I put on my slippers—*ains, zvei, drei*,[19]
While Bubbie enjoyed her herring and rye.

I grabbed for my bathrobe and buttoned my *gotkies*.[20]
Bubbie was busy devouring the *latkes*.[21]

1. *Chanukah:* an eight-day Jewish holiday starting on the 25th of the month of Kislev.
2. *Boichecks* and *maidels:* boys and girls.
3. *Draidels:* wooden toys that make a loud clacking noise when spun in the hand.
4. *Menorah:* a candelabrum whose candles are lit during Jewish services.
5. *Bubbie:* grandmother.
6. *Glassele tay:* glass of tea.
7. *Zoyereh:* sour.
8. *Oi vei!:* an expression of sorrow.
9. *Gesundt:* healthy; also an exclamation meaning "Good health."
10. *Geshmack:* delicious or tasty (refers to "taiglach").
11. *Kinderlach:* little children.
12. *Taiglach:* small cakes filled with nuts and fruits and dipped in honey.
13. *Chanukah gelt:* Chanukah gifts of money.
14. *Kluppen* and *ticken:* knocking and ticking.
15. *Shtickele:* little piece (of).
16. *Tummel:* tumult, noise, commotion.
17. *Beruches:* blessings.
18. *Tuchis:* rear end.
19. *Ains, zvei, drei:* one, two, three.
20. *Gotkies:* underwear.
21. *Latkes:* pancakes.

To the window I ran, and to my surprise,
A little red *yarmulke*[22] greeted my eyes.

When he got to the door and saw the Menorah,
"Yiddishe kinder," he said, *"Kenahorah.*[23]

"I thought I was entering a different *hoise,*[24]
But as long as I'm here, I will leave a few toys."

"Come into the kitchen," said I, "for a dish.
Here's a *gupel*, a *lefel*, and a *shtickele* fish."[25]

With smacks of delight, he started his *fressen,*[26]
Chopped liver and *knaidlach*[27] and *kreplach*[28] *gegessen.*[29]

Along with his meal he had a few *schnappes.*[30]
When it came to his eating, this fat boy was tops.

He asked for some *knishes*[31] with pepper and salt,
But they were so hot that he yelled, *"Oy gevalt!"*[32]

He buttoned his *hoysen* and ran from the *tish.*[33]
"Your *koshereh*[34] meals are simply delish."

As he went through the door, he said, "See ya-all later.
I'll be back next *Pesach*[35] in time for the *Seder.*"[36]

More rapid than eagles his prancers they came,
As he whistled and shouted and called them by name.

22. *Yarmulke:* skullcap.
23. Translated: "Jewish children," he said, "may no evil befall you."
24. *Hoise:* house.
25. Translated: "Here's a fork, a teaspoon, and a piece of fish."
26. *Fressen:* to devour like a glutton.
27. *Knaidlach:* dumplings.
28. *Kreplach:* square or triangular dumplings filled with ground meat or cheese.
29. *Gegessen:* in this context, "to eat."
30. *Schnappes:* small drinks of liquor.
31. *Knishes:* small round or square lumps of dough stuffed with filling.
32. *Oy gevalt!:* an all-purpose exclamation of fear, astonishment, horror, dismay, frustration; equivalent to "My God!"
33. Translated: "He buttoned his pants and ran from the table."
34. *Koshereh:* kosher.
35. *Pesach:* Passover.
36. *Seder:* ceremonial dinner held on the first evening of Passover.

"Now Izzie! Now Morris! Now Louis! and Sammy!
On Irving and Maxie! and Hymie and Mannie!"

He gave a *geshrei*[37] as he drove out of sight.
"Good *yontiff*[38] to all and to all a good night!"

Der Nighd Pehind Grisdmas

by Sidney W. Wetmore

Years ago I tore this out of an old paperback collection titled *Comic Recitations.* I no longer have the book, so I don't know who edited it, when or by whom it was published, or anything about the poem's author. I don't even know what the speaker's native language is.

'Tvas der nighd pehind Grisdmas, und all ofer der haus,
Nod von beobles vas schleebing, nix cum arous;
Dea sdockings vas vlung all ofer dose shair,
Vor hopes auf Saind Niglebus nix longer vos dhere,
Yimmie und Shakey vas tossing widoud schleeb in der ped,
Der leddle stomachs vas pig, wid gandy, nuds, bies and
    pread
Vhile mudder mit a nighd-dress, und I mit a gown,
Vas yust make up our minds ve couldn't lie down;
Ven vrom der haus oud py der lawn ve heard somedings
    gletter,

37. *Geshrei:* a scream or shout.
38. *Yontiff:* holiday.

Like der tuyfle I shumped ofer my shair, vonderin' vat vas
    der madder.
Righd avay qvick to der vinder I vent, vith a vlash,
Grapped avay der plinds und shofed up der sash;
Der moon, all undressed, vas foolin' arount pelow,
Und saying, "Gife us a rest, mit dat 'Peautiful Schnow.''
Vat vas dose, so hellup me, vibeh to dhese eyes appear,
Bud a horse and schleigh, poth vas oldt und qveer,
Trawin a leddle oldt bump-packed rooster, solemn and
    schlow,
Dot I know'd mit a glance 'twas oldt Toctor Prough.
Vrom der oudside I drew my head, und durnt arounts,
Ven up-stairs comes dot rooster, mit dwo or dhree pounts;
He vas all govered up mit a pig ofergoat made long pelow,
Und der vhisker py hes schin vas vhide like der schnow;
He spoke nix a vord, bud straighd vend to vork,
Velt all der bulses, und gifer der arms a jerk;
Und making hes vingers on der top of hes nose,
Vith a vag auf hes ear, to der schminey he goes;
"Vod sboonful of oil, oldt vomans, und sum prandy,
Scheese dose nuts, raisins, bies und der gandy:
Dose dender schmalt stomach vill nefer digest
Der schveets vot dhey get—pretzels und krout vas der feast."
Bud dat makes nodhings out, does advice mit vrents.
Ven der gustom auf Grisdmas der odeer vay dends;
All vater und muttors, old Schanty Claws too,
Vas oxceeding plind; vell, a goot-nighd to you.
Und dhese vords ve heard him exclaim, as he trofe oud auf
    sighd,
"Dose bully bies, raisins, und gandy makes toctor's bill all
    righd."

Adobe Joe's Christmas

by Peter H. Eichstaedt

In my collection are several parodies in Spanish dialect that go back at least to the 1950s. They are not included here because they contain lines that might offend Spanish readers. The most popular of such parodies, sent to me in typescript form by several friends (no two versions of the poem exactly alike) opens:

'Tis the night before Christmas and all through *la casa*
Not a creature is stirring. *¡Caramba! ¿Qué pasa?*
[How strange! What is going on?]

The following parody, with its introductory paragraphs, is by Peter Eichstaedt, a senior reporter on the *New Mexican*, a Santa Fe, New Mexico, newspaper. It appeared in that paper on the day before Christmas, 1989.

A cold wind blew under a grey sky as I drove out to the small ranch house of my old friend, Adobe Joe.

I knew I was doing the right thing taking him to my house. It was Christmas eve and I couldn't stand the thought of Joe spending that time alone. After all he had gotten a broken foot several weeks ago when a horse had stepped on him.

I thought Joe was quiet on the way in to my house, but then I didn't blame him. It was the time of year to get mellow, or even nostalgic.

Inside the house Joe's spirits picked up. It could have been the warmth of the fire, the smell of enchiladas in the oven or the kids' excitement.

Joe was helpful and convinced the kids to go to bed, saying he would tell them a special story if they went to sleep. He hobbled down the hall and sat on the edge of a bed while I listened in.

'Twas the night
Before Christmas
And all *en la casa*[1]
Not a critter was stirring,
In fact *nada pasa.*[2]

The socks, they were hung
By the fireplace with care,
And we all hoped to ourselves
Santa soon would be there.

Los niños[3] were snoozing
Two to a *cama*[4]
And dreaming of good things
They'd find *la mañana.*[5]

But me and Rosita
Hadn't done much smiling.

No hay[6] work in the winter
And the bills just kept piling.

Then out on the road
I heard a deep rumble,
I choked on my beer and
Figured here's trouble.

La luna[7] was shining
On the crunchy white *nieve.*[8]
It lit up the night
Almost like day.

I couldn't believe
What I saw when I saw it;
A 4-wheel highrider with
Big tires and antlers.

1. *En la casa:* in the house.
2. *Nada pasa:* nothing was moving.
3. *Los niños:* the children.
4. *Cama:* bed.

5. *La mañana:* tomorrow.
6. *No hay:* there is no.
7. *La luna:* the moon.
8. *Nieve:* snow.

The driver was hidden
Behind the windshield,
When he grated the gears,
The fanbelt squealed.

He slid down the *arroyo*[9]
Without any trouble
And climbed the other side
In low gear *muy pronto.*[10]

The truck bed was piled
With presents so high,
I squinted and wondered
Diablos!,[11] who's this guy?

He climbed down from the cab
Knee deep in the snow,
With a sack full of toys;
Said, "Wha's happenin', Bro?"

He wore jeans and boots,
A plaid shirt and dark glasses,
A stocking cap on his head
And giant mustaches.

He came right inside,
And quickly got busy,

Setting up toys and dolls;
It all made me dizzy.

He paused for a minute,
Because he was cold,
And stood by the fire
Before hitting the road.

He saw the red chile,
Frijoles y posole,[12]
And helped himself to chips
And green *guacamole.*[13]

Then with a small burp
He wiped his mustaches,
And used his shirt
To polish his glasses.

Then he hustled outside
Without saying his *nombre;*[14]
Started the engine and said,
Mil gracias, hombre!"[15]

Then over the rumble
And shifting of gears,
I heard him shout out
"Feliz Navidad[16]
y Happy New Year!"

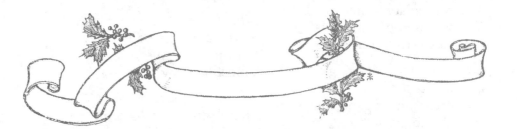

9. *Arroyo:* small river.
10. *Muy pronto:* very quickly.
11. *Diablos!:* the Devil!
12. *Frijoles y posole:* beans and barley.
13. *Guacamole:* alligator pear salad, a Cuban dish.

14. *Nombre:* name.
15. *Mil gracias, hombre:* a thousand thanks, man
16. *Feliz Navidad:* a felicitous Christmas.

Pancho Claus

by Lalo Guerrero

These are the lyrics of a song written in 1955 and recorded
by the late Jacqueline McCarty, a Santa Fe woman who sang
under the name of La Gringa. The author, Lalo Guerrero,
now heads his own publishing company, Barrio Libre
Music—BMI, in San Bernardino, California.

'Twas the night before Christmas,
And all through the *casa*,[1]
Mama, she was busy preparing the *masa*,[2]
To make the tamales for the *tamalada*,
And all the ingredients for the enchiladas.

Papa in the front room with all the *muchachas*[3]
Was dancing the mamba and doing the cha-cha.
My brothers and sisters were out in the hall
Listening to Elvis sing hard rock n' roll.

When all of a sudden, I heard such a racket,
I jumped out of bed and put on my jacket.
I went to the window, and in front of the house
Was my old Uncle Pedro, as drunk as a louse.
He ran in the house and he grabbed the *guitarra*.[4]
He let out a yell and he sang "Guadalajara."[5]

I was starting to wonder, as I lay there alone,
How old Santa Claus was to visit my home.
With all of this noise, they would scare him away,
When all of a sudden, I heard someone say,

1. *Casa:* house.
2. *Masa:* dough.
3. *Muchachas:* girls.
4. *Guitarra:* guitar.
5. "Guadalajara": a popular Spanish song.

"Hey! Pablo! Chuchito! Gordito! José!
Get up there, you bums, or you don't get no hay!"

And what to my wondering eyes did appear,
But eight little donkeys, instead of reindeer.
And they pulled a *carreta*[6] that was full of toys
For all of us good little girlies and boys.
The fat little driver waved a big sombrero,
And said, "Merry Christmas, *Feliz Año Nuevo.*"[7]
I heard him exclaim, as he rode past the porches,
"Merry Christmas to all, and to all *buenos noches!*"[8]

6. *Carreta:* cart.
7. *Feliz Año Nuevo:* Happy New Year.
8. *Buenos noches:* Good night.

Da Night Before da Christmas

by Kevin Scannell

The Upper Peninsula of Michigan, abbreviated U.P., is close
to Canada and almost like a separate state. It was settled
mostly by Scandinavians and Finns who speak in a dialect
all their own. Michigan residents below the peninsula call
them Yoopers. There are Yooper songs, Yooper jokes, and
even Yooper bumper stickers, such as the one that says: "Say
ya to the Upper Peninsula, eh?" (Yoopers say "ya" for "yes,"
and like to end sentences with "eh?")

Keven Scannell, of Escanaba, Michigan, is the author
of this parody, written in Yooper dialect. He is program
director and morning announcer of Escanaba's radio station
WDBC.

'Twas da night before Christmas and all troo da U.P.
Not a Yooper was eating, not even a pasty.[1]
—As you's can see, I'll be stretching my poetic license to da
     limit on
Dis one. . . . Anyways
Da flannel shirts were hung by da sauna wid care
In hopes dat Saint Nick would soon be dare.
Da liddle ones were nestled all snug in dare beds
While visions of *ludefisk*[2] swam in dare heads.
And mama in her long-johns and I in my *chook*[3]
Had just settled our bellies after a plate of chinook,[4]
When out on da lawn dare was dis big sound.
I jumps out a bed to see wad da heck's goin on.
And out on my front lawn so early in da morn
Is dis small pick-up truck and eight tiny spikehorn[5]
—You see, Santa's on a budget dis year. . . . Anyways
Da little old driver, so lively and quick,
I knews right dare it must be St. Nick.
Faster dan smelt in spring day came
And he huffed and puffed and called dem by name:
"Now Toivo, Now Aino, Now Sulo and Arvo,
On Larry, On Daryl, On da udder deer Daryl.[6]
To da top of da porch to da top of da wall,
Now dash away dash away dash away all."
I's looks back in cause I's hears dis big sound.
Down da chimney St. Nick comes wid a bound.
His eyes, day did twinkle, his dimples so merry,
His nose was red, probably just came from Trenary.[7]
Da stump of a pipe he held tight in his teeth,
And da smoke it encircled his head like a wreath.

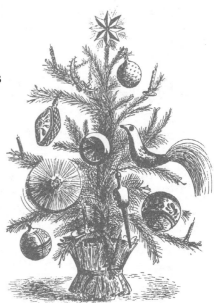

1. Pasty: a meat pie special to the area.
2. *Ludefisk:* whitefish soaked in brine and dried out. It smells awful. Many
grocery stores in the area carry it only during the Yuletide holidays.
3. *Chook:* a stocking cap.
4. Chinook: a type of salmon found in the Great Lakes.
5. Spikehorn: reindeer.
6. Other Daryl: a reference to the two Daryl brothers in the Bob Newhart
television comedy show.
7. Trenary: a village near Escanaba, known for its hospitable bars.

He has dis broad face and a round little belly
Dat shook when he laughed like a bowlful of jelly.
Dis guy's gots a belly, a red nose, and he smokes . . .
    somebody should
Checks his blood pressure. . . . Anyways . . .
He doesn't say a ting, just does his job,
And fills all da socks wid corn on da cob.
He sprang to his truck and tells his spikehorns to go,
And away day all flew like it was da middle of hunting
    season.
But I heards him say as he drove troo da air,
"Happy Christmas, Yoopers," and to all a big "Hey dare!"

Get With It, Santa Baby

by Sandra Rokoff

Sandra Rokoff is the author of six books for children, in-
cluding *The Mission of Piades I, The Robber Child, I Can Fly an
Airplane,* and *There Are Lots of Ways to Grow, You Know.* Her
lively parody of Moore's poem was written while working
with eight boys in a special education class at one of Santa
Fe's junior high schools. The boys illustrated the poem for
the 1980 Adobe Christmas edition of the *Santa Fe Reporter.*
    Because slang has not changed much in the past decade,
I have not tried to explain all the terms except for a couple
that may not be clear to all readers.

'Twas the night before Christmas, when all through the
    "pad"
Not a "mousie" was stirring, and was our cat mad!
The "tube socks" were hung by the chimney with care
In hopes that the "Jolly Fat Dude" would be there.

The children were nestled all snug in their beds,
While visions of "munchies" danced round in their heads.
Then Ma turned the "tube" off (she'd been watching "MASH")
And said to me, "Pa, it's 10:30 . . . let's crash."

When out in the street there began such a racket,
I covered my ears 'cause I just couldn't "hack it."
Away to the window I flew like a bird
To see what was making those noises I'd heard.

The moon was so big that the whole yard appeared
As bright as at midday, and wow, was that weird!
But, what I saw down there . . . was real "heavy, man,"
On the snow was a miniature Chevrolet van!

With a little old "geezer" so lively and quick,
I knew in a moment it must be St. Nick.
His van was all pinstriped, with red lacquered flames,
And a mural of reindeer (including their names).

There was Dasher and Dancer and Prancer and Vixen,
Comet and Cupid and Donder and Blitzen.
To the top of the porch, 20 feet in the air,
With "savage" hydraulics, it hopped like a hare.

Then, as chrome mags and headers shone bright 'gainst the sky,
The tiny van started to "haul it" and fly!
To the top of the house it rose up in a poof,
With a bag full of toys popping from the sun roof.

And then in a twinkling, I heard up above,
The sound of that "wild crazy guy" we all love,
As I drew in my head and was turning around,
Down the chimney St. Nicholas came with a bound.

He was dressed in red "threads" from his head to his foot,
And his "savage" fur suit was all covered with soot.
His huge bundle of toys, I could see from afar,
Made him look like he must be as rich as J.R.![1]

1. J.R.: J. R. Ewing, of soap opera fame.

His cheeks were as pink as a rose on the vine,
And his nose was all red like he drank too much wine.
The beard on his chin was as white as the snow.
He stretched his hand toward me and said "Ese bro!"[2]

The stump of a pipe he held tight in his teeth
And the smoke, it encircled his head like a wreath.
I could tell that this "dude," with his fat little "pot,"
Had never been running or jogging a lot.

He was chubby and plump, a right jolly old elf.
I "cracked up" when I saw him, in spite of myself.
A wink of his eye and a nod of his head
Soon gave me to know I had nothing to dread.

He spoke not a word, but went on with his "trip"
Of filling the socks; then snapped round like a whip,
And laying a finger aside of his nose,
Gave a nod, and then, ZOOM! up the chimney he rose.

He climbed in his Chevy, his motor he started,
And then through the cold, wintry landscape he darted.
But I heard him shout back o'er the noise of his van,
"—MERRY CHRISTMAS TO ALL . . . AND TO YOU,
     LATER, MAN!"

Texas Night Before Christmas

by James Rice

James Rice, who lives in Hico, Texas, is one of the South's
leading illustrators of juvenile books. He has written and/or
illustrated more than twenty-five books, including an edition

2. Ese bro: my brother.

of Moore's original ballad. This and the following poem are from two books that he wrote and illustrated, published by Pelican in 1986. I have not included an earlier Texas parody, "The Night Before Christmas, in Texas, That Is," by Leon A. Harris, Jr. It was first published in 1952 by Lothrop, Lee and Shepard, and reissued in 1986 by Pelican.

'Twas the night before Christmas
　　in the cold wintry fog.
Nary a critter was movin',
　　nor a lone prairie dog.

Then from out of the north
　　the breeze gave a stir;
An icy cold blast
　　swirled the fog in a blur.

A blue Texas norther
　　roared over the plains.
The cold fairly whistled
　　through the loose winderpanes.

I poked at the farplace
　　to stir up a flame—
The embers glowed redder,
　　but the cold stayed the same.

Ma fixed up our dinner
　　to be ready next day
And thought about Christmas
　　a few hours away.

Our scuffed boots were assembled
　　on the floor pair by pair
Where Santy would find 'em,
　　for he soon would be there.

The younguns were bundled
　　down snug in their covers,
A sprout of a girl
　　and her two older brothers.

So me in my long johns
　　and Ma in her gown
Warmed up by the far
　　'fore we laid ourselves down.

Then from out on the range
　　there came such a ruckus,
I ran to the winder
　　to see what the fuss was.

Through the blue winter blizzard
　　a scene came to sight;
I squinted to see,
　　for there waren't much light.

There stompin' and snortin'
　　and pawin' the ground
Were eight scroungy longhorns
　　stampedin' around

In front of a wagon
　　piled full as could be
With boxes and bundles
　　as high as a tree.

Then a bellerin' yell
　　soon set them all straight
From a fat li'l ole ramrod[1]
　　who put fear in the eight.

Well, they waren't really scairt—
　　no harm would he cause—
For their longhorn head honcho
　　was old Santy Claus!

[1] Ramrod: the boss.

He got their attention
  and called them by name,
"Hey, Leadfoot and Waleye—
  git up there, Culhane!

"Come on, Gimp and Flopear
  and Scarface—start draggin',
Git on, Sam and High-Hips,
  let's move this here wagon!"

Old Leadfoot, he bellered
  and lifted his head,
Then straight on they trampled
  through Ma's flower bed.

They laid the gate flat,
  and the clothesline went, too.
Nothin' stood in their way
  as they flat-footed through.

Santy pulled them up short
  on top of the roof
After wrecking the porch
  with them clodhopper hoofs.

They rocked our sod shanty,
  the dirt sifted down,
And then through the chimney
  Santy came with a bound!

He was dressed all in rawhide
  with a Stetson on top.
His big Texas boots
  hit the floor with a clop.

He shook his great belly
  and stomped with each foot,
Which knocked off a shower
  of mud, ash, and soot.

His eyes were both squinty
  and his skin was like leather
From too much exposure
  to the raw Texas weather.

He looked tough as a horseshoe,
  but I felt no alarm,
'Cause a wink of his eye
  showed he'd do us no harm.

A feed bag of toys
  he flung from his back,
And with nary a word
  he opened the sack.

He filled all the boots
  and piled them up high,
Then looked out the winder
  and up at the sky.

The cold Texas norther
  still whistled and blew,
But more younguns was waitin'—
  his work wasn't through.

It was hard to just leave
  and walk through the door
To face all them longhorns
  and the cold as before.

He drank some hot mud
  and hunched close to the heat
To soak up the warmth
  and thaw his cold feet.

He could no longer dally
  or put off the chore,
So he gave us a wink
  and pushed through the door.

He prodded the longhorns
  to get on the go,
And the wagon took off
  through the fog and the snow.

He called over the norther
  'fore he went out of sight,
"Merry Christmas, y'heah?
  and y'all have a good night!"

Prairie Night Before Christmas

by James Rice

'Twas a cold Christmas eve
  on the Southwestern plain
And the North wind was blowin'
  through a broke winderpane.

In that sod shanty shack
  far from home, warmth and care
Shivered two lonely cowboys,
  such a scraggly pair.

They crowded the farplace
  where the flames flickered low
From smoldering embers
  that heated too slow.

Then a knock at the door
  and a bang on the wall—
Over the sound of the storm
  they heard a voice call,

"Please open the door
  and let me come in;
I'm near froze to death
  and chilled to the skin."

The door was unbolted
  and then opened wide
And a fat li'l ole man
  jumped quickly inside.

There was frost on his whiskers
  and ice hung from his nose;
He shivered and shook
  from his head to his toes.

In spite of discomfort
  he didn't complain.
His expression was jolly
  as he paused to explain,

"I was movin' this cargo
  and making good time;
I'd covered the country
  from desert to pine,

"Till I crossed the border
  to this panhandle land
And a Southwestern norther
  commenced stirring the sand.

"The temperature dropped
  more'n a hunnert degrees;
My team soon fled North
  where they'd less likely freeze."

The old cowman had doubts
  'bout the strange little man
But in Southwest tradition
  he put out his hand.

"You can shake off your boots;
  you're welcome to stay
Or we can help ya
  to be on your way."

The answer came quickly
  with a twinkle of eye,
"I got many a mile yet
  'fore the sun hits the sky.

"Could you find me a team
    (I gladly will pay)
Then point my nose South
    and I'll be on my way."

"The only critters we have
    that could pull a full load
Are the ornery longhorns
    and they'd have to be showed.

"They ain't ever been hitched
    to a wagon with reins;
They'd be too much trouble—
    they're a mite short on brains."

They made an odd threesome
    as they went out on the range—
The old cowhand and the youngster
    and the old man so strange.

They saddled three broncs
    in the dark freezing night;
With cold-stiffened fingers
    they made the cinch tight.

While roping the longhorns
    they bumped and they stumbled
And numerous times
    from their hosses they tumbled.

It took all three working
    an hour or more
To hitch up the wagon
    in two rows of four.

The longhorns at first
    refused to obey,
When the strange little man
    tried to get under way.

Then one lifted his head
    and gave out a bellow

And the rest one by one
    they started to follow.

The longhorns were straining
    and pulling together;
they built up their speed
    then just like a feather—

On a strong gust of wind
    their feet gave a bound
Then man, wagon and longhorns
    all at once left the ground!

The old cowboy and youngster
    stared up in surprise,
A trick of the storm,
    too much wind in the eyes—

Those were their thoughts
    as they looked at the sky;
Any fool knew darn well
    that such things cannot fly.

The young cowboy grumbled
    as they moved toward the shack,
But the old one stayed quiet
    pert' near all the way back.

They reached the sod shanty
    and opened the door
And they couldn't believe
    what they saw on the floor.

Two pairs of new boots
    with spurs made of silver,
With a note but no clue
    as to who was the giver.

They made out the words
    in the dim farplace light:
"MERRY CHRISTMAS TO ALL
    AND TO ALL A GOOD NIGHT!"

Cajun Night Before Christmas

by J. B. Kling, Jr.

Mr. Kling is a retired Baton Rouge, Louisiana, law-enforcement officer and popular after-dinner speaker. His Cajun version of Moore's ballad first appeared as a Christmas message from the Bergerson Printing Company of New Orleans under the pseudonym "Trosclair." Howard Jacobs adapted it for Pelican's best-selling book, illustrated by James Rice and published in 1973.

'Twas the night before Christmas
An' all t'ru de house
Dey don't a t'ing pass
Not even a mouse.
De chirren been nezzle
Good snug on de flo'
An' Mama pass de pepper
T'ru de crack on de do'.

Den Mama in de fireplace
Done roas' up de ham
Stir up de gumbo
An' make bake de yam.

Den out on de by-you
Dey got such a clatter
Make soun' like old Boudreau
Done fall off his ladder.

I run like a rabbit
To got to de do'
Trip over de dorg
An' fall on de flo'!

As I look out de do'

In de light o' de moon
I t'ink, "Manh, you crazy
Or got ol' too soon."

Cuz dere on de by-you
W'en I stretch ma' neck stiff
Dere's eight alligator
A pullin' de skiff.

An' a little fat drover
Wit' a long pole-ing stick
I know r'at away
Got to be ole St. Nick.

Mo' fas'er an' fas'er
De 'gator dey came
He whistle an' holler
An' call dem by name:

"Ha, Gaston!
Ha, Tiboy!
Ha, Pierre an' Alceé!
Gee, Ninette!
Gee, Suzette!
Celeste an' Reneé!

"To de top o' de porch
To de top o' de wall
Make crawl, alligator,
An' be sho' you don' fall."

Like Tante Flo's cat
T'ru de treetop he fly
W'en de big ole houn' dorg
Come a run hisse'f by
Like dat up de porch
Dem ole 'gator clim!
Wit' de skiff full o' toy
An' St. Nicklus behin'.
Den on top de porch roof
It soun' like de hail
W'en all dem big 'gator
Done sot down dey tail.

Den down de chimney
I yell wit' a bam
An' St. Nicklus fall
An' sit on de yam.
"Sacre!" he axclaim,
"Ma pant got a hole
I done sot ma'se'f
On dem red hot coal."

He got on his foots
An' jump like a cat
Out to de flo'
Where he lan' wit' a SPLAT!

He was dress in musk-rat
From his head to his foot
An' his clothes is all dirty
Wit' ashes an' soot.
A sack full o' playt'ing
He t'row on his back

He look like a burglar
An' dass fo' a fack.

His eyes how dey shine
His dimple, how merry!
Maybe he been drink
De wine from blackberry.
His cheek was like rose
His nose like a cherry
On secon' t'ought maybe
He lap up de sherry.

Wit' snow-white chin whisker
An' quiverin' belly
He shook w'en he laugh
Like de stromberry jelly!

But a wink in his eye
An' a shook o' his head
Make my confi-dence dat
I don' got to be scared.

He don' do no talkin'
Gone straight to his work
Put playt'ing in sock
An' den turn wit' a jerk.

He put bot' his han'
Dere on top o' his head
Cas' an eye on de chimney
An' den he done said:
"Wit' all o' dat fire
An' dem burnin' hot flame
Me I ain' goin' back
By de way dat I came."

So he run out de do'
An' he clim' to de roof

He ain' no fool, him
For to make one more goof.

He jump in his skiff
An' crack his big whip.
De 'gator move down

An' don' make one slip.

An' I hear him shout loud
As a splashin' he go
"Merry Christmas to all
'Til I saw you some mo'!"

Hillbilly Night Afore Christmas

by Thomas Noel Turner

A native of the Appalachian mountains, Thomas Noel Turner
is a professor of education at the University of Tennessee.
His parody (Pelican, 1983) is illustrated by James Rice.

'Twas the night afore Christmas
  'Twixt ridgeback and holler,
No critter was twitchin'
  Nary hawg dast to waller.

Each keerful darn't stockin'
  War' nail't near the chimbley,
A hopin' that Sainty'd
  Be a extry bit fren'ly.

The youngun's was snuggle't
  Grub deep in the tickin',
Dream conjurin' up or'nges
  And stripe't candy lickin'.

Ole Maw in her night dress
  And me in my long johns,

Wuz a snorin' es happy
  Es frogs in thuh lake ponds.

When up in the piney woods
  Come a scair't paint'er screechin',
Ain't heered sich a ruckus
  Since camp meetin' preachin'.

Wuz thet wu'thless houn', Blue,
  With a growl full of shiver,
Tried tuh crawl 'neath thuh bedstid,
  I th'owed off thuh kivver.

I grabb't fer my rifle gun,
  'Most farred hit off too,
Then tremblin' in sock feet
  Near tripp't on ole Blue.

Aire plank door creaked dreadful
  Jist op'nin' a mite,
So's I knowed flat out sartin
  Ha'nts walked th'ew thuh night.

They's a bright punkin' moon
  Tuh bring moonshiners sorrah,
Made it middle day brightness
  Like thuh woods wuz a-far.

Kindly dreamy, way yonder,
  Pure floatin' up aire,
Come a ole timey wagon
  And eight smokey bear.

With a sawed off ole peddler
  As quick as a bainty,
Hit whomped like a mule kick,
  Thet had to be Sainty.

To beat hummin' birds' wings
  Thet bear passel came,
Whilst he growled, "Gee!" then "Haw!"
  Es he hollered the'r names.

"On, Big Feet! On, Orn'ry!
  "Molasses an' Rumbler!
"Up, Yowler! Up, Growler!
  "On, Gumption an' Grumbler!

"Git over thet hinhouse!
  "Light out to the shed!
"Now climb, you ole honey bears!
  "Jist mind what I said!"

Es biddies fum sarpents
  Ur Maw's stripe't cat,
Fluster which way to go,
  Firstly this'n, then that.

So's up to the tin roof
  Them spry varmints clumb,
With a good few of purties
  And ole Sainty, by gum.

And d'recly I heered
  Sich a turrible trompin',
Like'n hail big es bisquit bread,
  Ur store teeth a chompin'.

Though I near met myself,
  Tarn'ed quick es a toad,
Sainty skinned down that chimbley
  'Fore I ever knowed.

He wuz snortin' and fussin',
  Stompin' snow fum his feet,
Breshin' off suht leavin's
  Whut stuck tuh his seat.

He'd a mouth made fer smiles
  Twicet too big fer elf-size,
A red jelly bean nose
  An' shoe button eyes.

His britches and coat,
  Wuz pure worryation,
Of quiltin' piece patches
  Tuh beat all creation.

He wore 'spenders and belt
  Like a man wif' a callin',
Tuh persactly be sartain
  His paints wuzn't fallin'.

You could tell he liked vittles
  Like stack cake and spoon bread,
An' al'ays tuk seconts
  When seconts wuz fed.

He'd granpappy whiskers,
  But his twinkledy eyes
Made him look like a youngun
  Whose smile never lies.

He looked plumb full of happy,
  Bof' cheeks puff't out wide,
Like a chaw of terbacky
  Wuz helt in each side.

A burn't black ole corn cob
  He 'peared 'bout to swaller,
Ever which way he goed
  Thuh smoke seem't tuh foller.

He'd shouldered a tote
  Stuffed to make yur eyes shine,
Made him out sum ole trapper
  A-tendin' his line.

He squinched up one eye,
  Give a "How d'ye do" grin,
Not a orphin nur widder
  Coulda been ascairt then.

He wuz more do than talk,
  To his chores bent his back,
Stuffed them stockin's right quick
  An' then heffed that there sack.

Then a pintin' me hush
  'Til my "Set a spell" friz,
With a meetin' house nod
  Out'n thuh chimbley he riz.

To his wagon he scrambled
  Real squirrely an' spritely,
Whupped them ole bears
  Kinda soft an' perlitely.

They lit out a bellerin'
  Like scairt scalded pups,
Ole Sainty, red wagon,
  An' smokey bear cubs.

But I give him a holler
  Afore he got clear,
"Merry Christmas, ole boy,
  "Y'all come back, yuh hear!"

TEN

High Life Below Stairs, by Robert Cruikshank

CURIOUS PARODIES

Santa Claus and Jenny Lind

by Anonymous

Jenny Lind (1820–1887), the world-famous Swedish coloratura soprano known as "the Swedish Nightingale," was brought to the United States by P. T. Barnum, the circus showman, for a triumphal two-year tour that made her name a household word. She later made her permanent home in England.

This ballad about her adventures with Santa was published as a small book, circa 1850, by John R. M'Gown and Company, 56 Ann Street, New York. Some of the illustrations are signed W. & J. T. Howland. One of the few known extant copies is owned by Betsy Shirley, who kindly photocopied the pages for me.

I don't know quite what to make of this puzzling, crudely written ballad. The start of Miss Lind's tour was in 1850, so the book was obviously intended to coincide with the excitement it generated. Thomas Nast had not yet established Santa as a fat man with a white beard, and the book's pictures show him as a clean-shaven gentleman in colonial dress. He seems to be some sort of benevolent warlock who rides the air on a broom, like Italy's good witch Befana, and can, if he likes, take the form of a young boy.

I'm a jolly old man, full of mirth and of cheer,
I never do sleep, for me that would be queer:
In summer, in winter, in autumn and spring,
O'er mountain and valley, I dance and I sing.

One day in the spring, it was pleasant and fair,
I stopped in a garden to see what was there;
The prettiest flowers I ever did see,
Grew near where I stood by the side of a tree.

Then a beautiful girl, and a fine looking boy,
Came out in the garden, themselves to enjoy;
They picked pretty flowers, their vases to fill,
And I flew away over valley and hill.

One day I was thinking—said I to myself,
I'll dress like a boy and be off like an elf:
Then I stopped in a house, myself to enjoy
With a gentleman, ladies, two girls and a boy.

"Come here," said one lady, "oh! do come to me,
You're the prettiest boy I ever did see."
I had nought on my head, not even a cap,
So I ran to the lady and jumped on her lap.

She told me a story, she sang me a song,
They were pretty, and funny, and not very long;
But I wiggled, and wriggled—I could n't keep still,
And then I was off, over mountain and hill.

On December 13, St. Lucia's day, Swedish girls wearing crowns of lighted candles present St. Lucia cakes to members of the household.

DRAWING BY FRITZ VAN DARDEL, COURTESY NORDIC MUSEUM, STOCKHOLM

I stopped at a church, and stood on the steeple,
I looked down below to see all the people;
Some gentlemen, ladies, and children were there,
A black man, with crutches and dark curly hair.

The black man was sitting—the others all stood;—
He was ragged and lame, and wanted some food;
A rosy-cheeked boy, with a cap on his head,
Said, "Here is some money, to buy you some bread."

I was happy to see such a good little boy,
And took from my pocket a beautiful toy:
I shouted and threw it, I could n't keep still,
And then I was off, over valley and hill.

Then I came to a place—I do not know where;
I could n't see well; there was smoke in the air:
At a distance I saw a very old house;
The girl with a hoop seemed as large as a mouse.

I stopped for a moment, just up in the air,
And I looked down below, to see what was there:

A bright little boy, with a beautiful cap,
Sat there on the ground with a dog on his lap.

I thought he was sick, for he looked very sad;
So I said to the boy, "My dear little lad,
Here's a very fine present, 't will cure you of pain;"
And then I was off over mountain and plain.

I stopped at a place where I saw many things:
A man with an apron without any strings;
A glass and a table, a lamp and some chairs;
And two or three men were just going up stairs.

On the steps of the house an old woman sat,
And there stood a man with a shiny new hat.
The boy with a dog was so full of his fun,
He shouted and laughed when the monkey did run.

The monkey jumped up by a man very black;
He ran round behind him to get on his back.
I could n't help laughing to see his long tail,
And then I flew off over mountain and dale.

When singing, and dancing, and dashing along,
I heard pretty music—it was not a song:
I stopped for a moment to look down below,
And there was a boy with his fiddle and bow.

Men, women and children were standing around,
And a little black dog sat there on the ground;
An old man with a staff, who seemed to be sad,
With his hat in his hand, stood near by the lad.

I quickly perceived that the poor man was blind—
The people around him seemed pleasant and kind:
They threw him some presents, his pockets to fill,
And I flew away over valley and hill.

Ha! ha! do you see that Old Santa is here?
My pockets are full, and I know I look queer.
The week before Christmas I gather my toys,
Most beautiful presents for girls, and for boys.

One pocket I fill with some books, very nice;

They tell pretty stories—I heed not the price.
The other I fill with toys, candies, and cake;
You'll jump up to get them as soon as you wake.

'T is a time to be merry—a time for good cheer,
When Santa comes round at the close of the year.
With many fine presents your stockings I'll fill,
And then I'll be off over mountain and hill.

The night before Christmas, while riding along,
I listened a moment to hear a sweet song;
I flew down a chimney on wings of the wind,
And there, just before me, sat Miss Jenny Lind.

I felt somewhat timid, but bowing quite low,
Said I, "Will Miss Jenny have me for a beau?
Come, ride with me, Jenny, and waken new joys—
Go sing for the children, while I give them toys."

She thought for a moment, and then she said, "Yes:"
She put on a cap and a new riding dress;
Then mounted behind me—the wind whistled shrill,
And we flew away over mountain and hill.

I'm a jolly old man—I ride in the wind;
The lady behind me is Miss Jenny Lind;
The horse that we ride is a broomstick, you see—
Oh! this is the horse for Miss Jenny and me.

With light airy wings it mounts up on the breeze,
And hastens away o'er the tops of the trees;
'T is swift as an arrow when shot from a bow;
It is up—it is off—how swiftly we go!

Cheer up, little children, do n't cry any more—
With many fine presents I'm now at your door—
Sing—sing for them, Jenny, oh, then they'll keep still,
And we will be off over valley and hill.

I left Jenny Lind in the valley below,
To sing for the children, and off I did go.
I'm a jolly old man—I could n't keep still—
And so I was off over valley and hill.

On the top of a mountain, where winds whistle bleak,
I am dancing a jig, I am having a freak;
I sing and am cheerful wherever I go;
I love the cold winter—the white drifting snow.

When out in the country I'm just like a boy;
The riding and skating I always enjoy.
I love to mount up on the swift-driving gale,
And hasten away over mountain and vale.

I'm cheerful and merry, though dancing alone,
On a happier man the moon never shone:
Just now I was thinking how funny 't would be,
If the boys and the girls were dancing with me.

Hurra for the girls and hurra for the boys,
Hurra for their pleasures and innocent joys,
Hurra for the mountain, all covered with snow,
Hurra for the breezes, wherever they blow.

I'm jolly and merry, and full of my glee;
I sing and I dance, I am happy and free;
I laugh at the frost, and I ride on the wind:
But I must return and get Miss Jenny Lind.

Ha! ha! Jenny Lind, I am with you again;
I've been far away over valley and plain:
I whistled and sang, I was happy and free,
I danced on the mountain, and had quite a spree.

While thinking, and winking, and dashing away,
I passed by a river and over a bay;
Then mounting up higher, I looked down below,
And saw the White Mountains all covered with snow.

Now hop up, Miss Jenny, and jump on behind;
Be pleasant and cheerful, I know you are kind:
The winds are awake, and I cannot stop long;
I'm off with my presents, and you with your song.

My dear little girls, do n't be jealous and sad,
I'm sure you will soon be quite happy and glad;
For I am not married to Jenny—oh! no:
She scarce would accept me one night for a beau.

She has a kind heart, and she loves to do good;
I told her a song would enliven the mood,
And all of the children most happy would be—
"Oh! then," said Miss Jenny, "I will go with thee."

Then quickly we mounted my swift-flying steed,
And were off over mountain, o'er forest and mead.
Sing, sing for them, Jenny, a sweet serenade,
And then we'll be off over mountain and glade.

Ha! ha! my dear children, are you all asleep?
I've come with my presents to give you a peep;
And Jenny is singing a beautiful song—
But wake, quickly wake, for we cannot stay long.

In villages, cities, and all the world o'er,
I fly down the chimney, and light on the floor;
While I fill the stockings, Miss Jenny doth sing,
In sweet warbling notes, like the birds of the spring.

Now we must be going, for morning draws near—
I'll come round again at the close of next year.
Sing, sing for them, Jenny, in notes soft and light:
Happy Christmas to all—to all a good-night!

The Knight Before Christmas

by Corinne Rockwell Swain

I do not know when this parody appeared in the humor magazine *Life*, nor do I have any information about the author. I found it in *Poems from "Life,"* edited by Oliver Herford and Charles Fields (Macmillan, 1923).

The knight, before Christmas, observed to his spouse,
"I'm charmed with the service, all over the house!
The cook offers daily my favorite dishes;
The butler's a wonder at guessing my wishes;
The steward's all ginger,[1] in spite of his years;
Wherever I glance, a retainer appears.
My barber excels in his deftness and speed;
The groom puts a satiny gloss on my steed;
My armor is scoured till it dazzles my sight,
My sword and my spear are abnormally bright.
The sentinels never are guilty of naps;
My varlets are constantly doffing their caps.
Dear Mother-in-law has abandoned her rages;
My squire alertly turns down the fresh pages.
Nurse Margery curtsies, the kitchen-wench bows;
The rustics raise marvelous porkers and cows.
My minstrel's loud carols resound with my fame;
The jester's quaint stories are never the same.
It's pleasant to note (though the date is but recent)
Our people all acting so awfully decent!
This shows us, my dear, that with common accord,
They're happy to serve so distinguished a lord."
But his lady replied, with a smile on her lips,
"The season approaches for holiday tips,
And your motto is plain, if you'll read it aright:
'Merry Christmas to all, and to all a good knight!' "

1. Ginger: spirited, energetic, plucky.

The Nocturnal Segment Preceding Yuletide

by Anonymous

I have several slightly different versions of this retelling of Moore's ballad in academic prose jargon. The earliest is from an obscure newsletter called *Drivel and Dross* (Vol. 1, No. 3, circa 1973) that circulated underground among magicians. The parody is given the pseudonymous byline of Lon Hackensacker, a name also used by the newsletter's shy editor. It is probably older than 1973. Can any reader tell me who wrote it?

'Twas the nocturnal segment of the diurnal period preceding the annual
  Yuletide celebration, and throughout our place of residence,
Kinetic activity was not in evidence among possessors of the potential,
  Including that species of domestic rodent known as *Mus Musculus*.

Hosiery was meticulously suspended from the foremost perimeter of the
  Woodburning caloric apparatus pursuant to our anticipatory pleasure
Regarding an imminent visitation from an eccentric philanthropist among
  Whose folkloric appellations is the honorific title of *St. Nicholas*.

The prepubescent siblings were comfortably ensconced in
their particular
Accommodations of subliminal repose and relaxation,
As subconscious hallucinations of variegated fruit confec-
tions moving
Rhythmically through their respective cerebrums were
made manifest.

My conjugal partner and I, attired in our nocturnal head
coverings, were
About to take advantage of the hibernal darkness when
suddenly, upon
The avenaceous exterior portion of the surrounding grounds,
there ascended
A cacophony of dissonance sufficient to induce anxiety and
apprehension.

The decibelic intensity was such, I felt compelled to arise
with alacrity
From my place of repose to ascertain the precise source
thereof.
Hastening to the casement, I forthwith opened the barriers
sealing this
Fenestration and perceived thereupon the lunar brilliance
without.

Said brilliance, reflecting on the surface of a crystalline down-
fall of
Frigid precipitation, might be said to rival that of the solar
meridian.
The reflection, aforementioned, permitted my incredulous
optical sensory
Organs to behold a miniature airborne runnered structure
of conveyance.

It was drawn by eight diminutive specimens of the genus
Rangifer and was
Piloted by a miniscule, aged chauffeur so ebullient and
nimble that it
Became instantly apparent that he was indeed our anticipated
caller

Arriving in the Nick of time (if I may beg propitiation for
the pun).

With his ungulate motive power travelling at what may have
been more
Vertiginous velocity than patriotic predators, he vocifer-
ated loudly,
Expelled breath musically through contracted labia, and ad-
dressed each of
The octet by his or her cognomen: "Now Dasher, now
Dancer . . ." et al.

He guided them to the uppermost exterior level of our abode
through which
Structure I could readily distinguish the concatenation of
two-to-the-fifth
Cloven pedal extremities. Forthwith, I retracted my cranium
from its
Erstwhile location and performed a one-hundred-eighty
degree pivot.

With utmost celerity, our distinguished visitant achieved
entry by way of
The smoke passage via a gingerly executed downward
leap.
He was clad in animal pelts soiled by the ebon residue from
oxidations of
Carboniferous fuels which had accumulated upon the
walls thereof.

I attributed his resemblance to a street vendor largely to the
plethora of
Assorted playthings which he bore dorsally in a commo-
dious cloth reticule.
His orbs were scintillant with reflected luminosity while his
submaxillary
Dermal indentations gave every indication of engaging
amiability.

The capillaries of his malar and nasal appurtenance were
engorged with
Blood which suffused the subcutaneous layers thereof.

The former approximated the coloration of Albion's floral
emblem while
The latter was reminiscent of the *Prunus Avium* or sweet
cherry.

His sub- and supralabials resembled nothing so much as a
common loop knot
And his ambient hirsute facial adornment appeared lik-
ened unto small
Tabular and columnar crystals of frozen water. Clenched
firmly between his
Incisors was a smoking piece, gray fumes from which
formed a tenuous ellipse.

The latter encircled his occiput in a manner such that would
suggest a
Decorative seasonal circlet of holly. His visage was wider
than it was
High and when he waxed audibly mirthful his corpulent
abdominal region
Undulated like impectinated fruit syrup in a hemi-spherical
container.

He was, in summary, neither more nor less than an obese,
jocund, multigenerian
Gnome, the optical perception of whom rendered me ris-
ibly frolicsome
Despite all concerted efforts to refrain from being so. He
rapidly lowered,
Then elevated one eyelid as he rotated his head slightly to
one side.

This coordinated activity on his part served to convey to me
the impression
That trepidation or apprehension on my part was totally
groundless.
Without utterance, and with dispatch, he commenced filling
the aforementioned
Hosiery with various articles of merchandise, also afore-
mentioned.

These he extracted with gusto from his dorsally transported
commodious

Cloth receptacle. Upon completion of this task, he cleanly executed an

Abrupt about-face, placed a single manual digit in lateral juxtaposition to
　His olfactory organ and inclined his cranium in a gesture of leave-taking.

Forthwith, he effected his egress by quickly renegotiating the smoke passage
　In reverse. He then propelled himself in a short vector onto his structure

Of conveyance and directed a musical expulsion of air through his contracted
　Oral sphincter to the antlered quadrupeds of burden.

He proceeded to soar aloft in a movement hitherto observable primarily
　Among the seed-bearing portions of a common weed. As his vehiculation

Progressed beyond the normal limits of visibility, there was absolutely
　No doubt that his parting exclamation was clearly audible, to wit:

"May there be made manifest an ecstatic yuletide to the planetary constituency
　And to that selfsame assemblage my most sincere and heartfelt wishes for a

Salubriously beneficial and gratifyingly pleasurable span of time subsequent
　To sunset and prior to dawn."

An Educator's Night Before Christmas

by Jean Horneck and Dorothy Waleski

This prose parody appeared in the *NEA* (National Education Association) *Journal*, December 1960. Its authors are from Rockville, Maryland.

W*hereas*, on an occasion immediately preceding the Nativity festival, throughout a certain dwelling unit, quiet descended, in which could be heard no disturbance, not even the sound emitted by a diminutive rodent related to, and in form resembling, a rat; and

Whereas, the offspring of the occupants had affixed their tubular, closely knit coverings for the nether limbs to the flue of the fireplace in expectation that a personage known as St. Nicholas would arrive; and

Whereas, said offspring had become somnolent, and were entertaining fantasies re saccharine-flavored fruit; and

Whereas, the adult male of the family, *et ux*, attired in proper headgear, had also become quiescent in anticipation of nocturnal inertia; and

Whereas, a distraction on the snowy acreage outside aroused the owner to investigate; and

Whereas, he perceived in a most unbelieving manner a vehicle propelled by eight domesticated quadrupeds of a species found in arctic regions; and

Whereas, a most odd rotund gentleman was entreating the aforesaid animals by their appellations, as follows: "Your immediate co-operation is requested. Dasher, Dancer, Prancer, and Vixen; and collective action by you will be much appreciated, Comet, Cupid, Donder, and Blitzen"; and

Whereas, subsequent to the above, there occurred a swift descent to the hearth by the aforementioned gentleman, where he proceeded to deposit gratuities in the aforementioned tubular coverings:

Now, therefore, be ye advised
That upon completion of these acts and his return to his original point of departure, he proclaimed a felicitation of the type prevalent and suitable to these occasions, i.e.,
Merry Christmas to All and to All a Good Night!

A Visit From St. Alphabet

by Dave Morice

This whimsical parody by an Iowa City writer, illustrator, and wordplay expert, first appeared in a booklet titled *A Visit from St. Alphabet*, written and illustrated by Mr. Morice. It was privately published in 1980 by The Toothpaste Press (it later changed its name to The Coffee House Press), West Branch, Iowa.

'Twas the night before X, when all through the Y
Not a letter was stirring, not even an I;
The S's were hung by the T's with care
In the hopes that St. Alphabet soon would be there;
The Z's were nestled all snug in their beds,
While visions of W's danced in their heads;
And U in your kerchief, and I in my cap,
Had just settled our words for a long writer's nap,—

When out on the paper there rose such a clatter,
I sprang from my sentence to see what was the matter.
Away to the period I flew like a flash,
Tore open the commas and threw up the dash.

The pen on the crest of the new-fallen O
Gave a lustre of adverbs to pronouns below;
When what to my wondering I's should freeze,
But a miniature A and eight tiny B's,

With a little word writer I never met—
I knew that it had to be St. Alphabet.
More rapid than pencils his pages they came,
And he wrote and typed, and called them by name:
"Now, P! now, O! now, E and T!
On, P! on, A! on, G and E!
To the top of the shelf, to the top of the wall!
Now tell away, yell away, spell away all!"

As dry leaves that before the wild W fly,
When they meet with a question-mark, mount to the sky,
So up to the bookshelf the pages they flew,
With the A full of nouns,—and St. Alphabet too.
And then in the books on the shelf I heard
The prancing and pawing of each little word.
As I drew in my ear, and was watching the sound,
Down the pages St. Alphabet came with a bound.

He was dressed all in A's from his B's to his C's,
And his D's were all tarnished with F's and G's;
A bundle of E's he had flung on his H,
And he looked like a poem just opening its page.
His I's, how they twinkled! his J's, how merry!
His K's were like roses, his L like a cherry;
His droll little M was drawn up like a bow,
And the N on his chin was as white as the O.

The stump of a P he held tight in his T,
And the Q it encircled his head like a V.
He had a broad R and a little curved S
That shook, when he laughed, in his anagrammed vest.
He was U! He was W! He was X, Y, and Z!
And I laughed, when I saw him, alphabetically.
A wink of his I and a twist of his J
Soon gave me to know he had nothing to say.

He spoke not a word, but went straight to his work,

And filled all the pages; then turned with a jerk,
And laying his pencil aside of his nose,
And giving a nod, up the pages he rose.
He sprang to his A, to his B's gave a C,
And away they all flew like the down of a Z;
But I read in the sky, ere he wrote out of sight,
"Happy Alphabet to all, and to all a good write!"

Santa and the Skull

by Zebina Frederick

A mosaic poem consists of lines from two or more poems
that are patched together to make a new poem. In earlier
periods it was called, in England, a *cento*, from the Greek

word for patchwork. Both the ancient Greeks and Romans wrote mosaic verse, and in the Middle Ages it was a common practice to patch together lines from ancient poems to produce devotional verse. Alexander Ross (1590–1654), a Scotsman, spent his life writing such whimsies. His masterpiece, "Virgilius Evangelizans," republished in 1769, was a life of Christ made up entirely of lines from Virgil!

All this comes by way of introducing a mosaic poem about Santa Claus that I came upon entirely by accident. On July 1, 1990, while browsing in an antique mall in Asheville, North Carolina, I opened an old book and out fell a yellowed newspaper clipping. The back bore a date of December 29, 1917, but there was no name of the paper or the town. The clipping reprinted the following letter from one Zebina Frederick:

Christmas eve I attended a feast, and after the feed a young woman recited two beautiful poems, one about war and the other about Santa Claus. I have been trying ever since to repeat them from memory, but cannot seem to get them just right. . . . I think I have them nearly correct, however. . . . Would you mind asking your readers to straighten them out for me, as I may want to recite them some day? The lines go, as I remember them:

'Twas the night before Christmas,
Old Kaspar's work was done;
Not a creature was stirring,
Not even a mouse was sitting in the sun.

The children were nestled all snug on the green,
And visions of sugar-plums danced through the head
Of his little grandchild, Wilhelmine.

When out on the lawn there arose such a clatter,
He sprang from his bed to see what was the matter,
And saw her brother Peterkin roll something large and
   round,
Which the moon on the breast of the new-fallen snow had
   found.

Old Kaspar took it from the boy who stood expectant by,
When what should appear to his wondering eye

But a miniature driver so lively and quick,
He knew in a minute it must be Saint Nick.

The old man shook his head
More rapid than leaves that before the wild hurricane fly.
" 'Tis some poor fellow's skull," he said,
"Who fell in the great victory."

Do you recognize the source of the alien lines? They are from Robert Southey's familiar poem "The Battle of Blenheim." Although a certain ingenuity was required to make the lines rhyme, this is one of the worst mosaic poems I have yet to encounter. However, when poetry is bad enough, it becomes amusing. That is why I have included this poem.

ELEVEN

RUDOLPH THE RED-NOSED REINDEER

Only one great addition has been made to our Santa Claus mythology since the days of Thomas Nast. I speak, of course, of Rudolph and his luminous nose. The story of how this came about is worth telling in detail.

It all began in 1939 when Robert Lewis May (1905–1976), a Phi Beta Kappa graduate of Dartmouth (class of 1926), was an advertising copywriter at the Chicago headquarters of Montgomery Ward. According to *Newsweek* (December 7, 1964) Ward's sales manager reminded May that for years at Christmas time the store had been giving "crummy little nothings" to its customers. Could he think of something less crummy? Here is what May said went through his mind:

First I decided that . . . nuts! . . . for Christmas, there was only one animal. No matter what, it had to be a reindeer. But I needed a reindeer who was different from the rest—an ugly-duckling type, one that children could identify themselves with vicariously.

An analysis of Santa Claus's needs in reindeer came down to strength, fast running, and the ability to fly in bad weather in dark, wintry skies. I knew I was getting close. Then . . . I had it! A nose . . . to shine in the dark and light the way, a big, red, shiny nose.

May's sequel to Moore's ballad has the same meter and rhymed couplets as the original. At first he called his reindeer Rollo, but at the last minute he changed the name to Rudolph. The thirty-eight-page booklet, illustrated by Denver Gillen (Applewood Books reprinted it in 1990), was an immediate hit with Ward shoppers. More than two million copies were given away that Christmas. In 1946, after the war and its paper shortage ended, Ward distributed more than three million new copies. That same year Sewell Avery, chairman of Montgomery Ward, generously gave the book's copyright to May. Maxton and Company, a small Chicago publisher of children's books (now a part of Follett), brought out an edition in 1947 that sold 100,000 copies in two years.

"Everything connected with Rudolph has a touch of miracle about it," May told *Newsweek*. The second miracle happened in 1949. John ("Johnny") David Marks, a highly successful songwriter living in New York City's Greenwich Village, was married to May's sister. Marks was a Phi Beta Kappa graduate of Colgate University and later served on the university's Board of Trustees. During World War II he commanded the 16th Special Service Company, leading it across Europe as part of General Patton's Third Army. Hit recordings of his songs had been made by such artists as Bing Crosby, Eddy Duchin, the Ink Spots, Sammy Kaye, Guy Lombardo, Glenn Miller, and Fats Waller.

Intrigued by his brother-in-law's tale, Marks wrote a song that retold Rudolph's story in a mere 113 words. It was recorded by the singing cowboy, Gene Autry, for Columbia Records. At first Autry thought it was an unseemly song for a cowboy, but his wife persuaded him to record it anyway.

Soon the song was number one on the Hit Parade, and millions more of May's book were sold. May left Montgomery

Ward in 1951 to handle Rudolph-related books, movies, comic strips, and hundreds of licensed products, including tea sets, stuffed animals, toy banks, flashlights, jigsaw puzzles, clocks, cookie cutters, clothing, pull toys and countless other items. Comic strips about Rudolph were syndicated in twenty-five countries. By 1964 the original book had topped twenty-five million sales in a variety of editions—hardcover, paperback, cloth (that young children could chew on), big and little Golden Books, a pop-up book, coloring books, and foreign translations. More than three hundred arrangements of Marks's song were made, and some forty million records sold.

An eight-minute animated color film about Rudolph was made in 1948 by Max Fleisher. Another animated story of

Rudolph was produced by Videocraft International in 1964. That same year Burl Ives sang the song and narrated the story on an NBC one-hour special sponsored by General Electric and featuring a complete musical score by Johnny Marks. It has been aired every Christmas since; indeed, it is the most often repeated TV special ever made. A film made by Rankin-Bass Productions, using animated stop-action puppets, was that company's first big success. It was followed by the same company's less successful *Rudolph's Shiny New Year*, narrated by Red Skelton and featuring another Marks song.

The story Burl Ives told on television concerns one of Santa's elves, who wants to be a dentist. The Abominable Snow Beast is the heavy. He kidnaps Rudolph and the reindeer's parents but eventually is knocked cold by the elf, who drops a large chunk of ice on the Beast's head and pulls his teeth while he is unconscious. No longer fearsome, the Beast turns into a nice fellow who goes to work for Santa. A big storm then threatens to cancel Santa's Christmas trip, but Rudolph's nose again saves the day.

Marks died in 1985, but his St. Nicholas Music Company still collects royalties every time "Rudolph" is played by a radio or television station, and in restaurants, bars, and shopping centers during the Yuletide season. Is there anyone who can't hum the tune and sing most of the lines? Johnny Marks wrote some nine hundred other songs, including such Christmas numbers as "When Santa Claus Gets Your Letter," "The Night Before Christmas," "A-Caroling We Go," "I Heard the Bells on Christmas Day," "Joyous Christmas," "Rockin' Around the Christmas Tree," "A Merry Merry Christmas," "Everyone's a Child at Christmas," and the ever-popular "Holly Jolly Christmas." But he is best remembered for his Rudolph song.

More than five hundred orchestras and singers have recorded it, including Bing Crosby, Perry Como, Mitch Miller, the Chipmunks, Paul McCartney, Ray Charles, Willie Nelson, Guy Lombardo, Lawrence Welk, Conway Twitty, the Temptations, and even Michael Jackson. The *New York Times* reported in 1985 that more than twelve million copies of the original Gene Autry recording had been sold. Total sales of all recordings are now over 150 million. The sheet music has topped eight million in sales of the standard arrangement, and twenty-five million of other arrangements.

A village called Rudolph, in central Wisconsin, claims to be the little reindeer's home town. Each year the post office there is inundated with requests for envelopes that the office rubber stamps in red ink with Rudolph's picture.

When *Newsweek* interviewed May in 1964, he was a middle management catalog editor at Montgomery Ward, the royalties from his book having more than paid for the education of his six children. That same year Follett brought out a new edition of the original booklet combined with *Rudolph Shines Again*, a sequel published by Follett in 1954 with pictures by Diana Magnuson. The sequel tells how Rudolph became depressed when his nose lost its shine. After he forgets about his nose in an unselfish and successful effort to find two lost baby rabbits, the glow returns, and just in time for him once more to help Santa make his rounds.

Almost nobody knows that in 1951, before he wrote *Rudolph Shines Again*, May composed an earlier sequel called *Rudolph's Second Christmas*. As far as I know, it was never printed, but in 1965 it was recorded by RCA as a record titled *Rudolph the Red-Nosed Reindeer*. The record features several Christmas songs, including the one by Johnny Marks, and a narration by Paul Wing of May's original ballad and its first sequel.

Rudolph's Second Christmas is told in prose, interrupted occasionally by anapestic couplets. While Rudolph is helping Santa read tons of letters from children (using his nose to light up the room during the North Pole's six months of darkness), he comes upon a letter so sad it makes him cry. Jimmy and Joan, two circus children, tell Santa they never get presents on Christmas because their father's circus keeps moving from town to town and Santa never finds them.

It is such a miserable little circus that its only animal is a toothless tiger who can't roar. Because it can't afford a man to be shot from a cannon, it shoots a mouse from a popgun instead. No town wants the circus to stay more than a day.

Rudolph manages to find the circus and talk to the children. On his way back to the North Pole, he stops to rest in a forest where he meets a group of bizarre animals. There is a turtle that runs as fast as a rabbit, and a rabbit that crawls like a turtle. A dog meows like a cat, and a cat barks like a dog. A canary talks like a parrot, and a parrot warbles like a canary. Other animals make fun of them, just as the other reindeer had made fun of Rudolph.

Rudolph has a wonderful idea. Why not have Santa take all these misfits to the circus? The plan is carried out, and the animals are a sensation. The circus becomes such a great success that it even hires a man to be shot from a cannon. Now the circus stays such a long time in the same town that come next Christmas Santa, with Rudolph again guiding his sleigh, has no trouble bringing gifts to Joan and Jimmy.

I'm surprised that this sequel, which I consider superior to *Rudolph Shines Again*, was never published as a children's book.

May died in Evanston, Illinois, in 1976. Like Clement Moore, he is remembered today for only one poem, of little aesthetic merit, that somehow captured the hearts of America.

If Moore's poem had never been published, and if someone today submitted it to a magazine or a juvenile book editor, would it be accepted? I doubt it. This is even more true of May's ballad. Margaret Sherwood Libby, in her *Book Week* column "For Boys and Girls" (December 13, 1964), reviewed the season's Christmas books. "The worst of the Santa books," she wrote, "is the oldest, a reissue for its 25th anniversary of that deplorably obvious popular verse, *Rudolph the Red-Nosed Reindeer*. . . . The routine rhymes, reusing many lines of Clement Moore, and the pictures, in the poorest Disney tradition, are not even lightened by the cheery pleasure of the tune." I suspect that every children's-book editor and librarian would agree with those sentiments.

It is an open secret in publishing circles that juvenile books are published primarily to please parents, who, of course, buy the books, and librarians, who account for the rest of the sales. As to what children actually like in prose, poetry, and art, many editors of children's books couldn't care less. Children prefer poetry that tells a simple story, with strong rhymes and clanking rhythms. They also prefer realistic pictures. Nothing bores children more than stories and poems about the wonders of nature, or art so distorted that they can't puzzle out what a picture is supposed to represent. This is precisely why the books children most adore, the Oz books for instance, are so often published by obscure houses after the big firms have rejected them as too out of line with current adult fashions.

We find this same snobbishness in Thomas Meehan's article, "Bah Humbug! To All Yule TV Kiddie Shows," in the *New York Times*, December 14, 1975. Meehan doesn't like any of them, and especially not the Burl Ives special about Rudolph. The fact that it is the longest-running, most-watched special in TV history, viewed every year in some eighteen million homes, means nothing to him. He calls it "utter claptrap—sentimental and inept schlock." On Christmas day, 1973, I heard Marks say on a radio interview that he continually got flack from teachers complaining of the way "history" is pronounced in the last line of his song.

May's two ballads are too long for this anthology. It is just as well, because it was the song, not May's poems, that made Rudolph so famous around the world. Through the generosity of Johnny Marks's son, Michael, I have permission to reprint the familiar lines.

And so it glows. Two ballads, close to doggerel, by two one-poem poets who lived a century apart, are now more firmly entrenched in our culture than the total output of Ezra Pound. Thousands of better crafted Christmas poems, some by eminent bards, lie buried under literary dust heaps. Learned critics may hold their noses, but Rudolph's red nose, thanks to Robert May and Johnny Marks, will be shining as long as Santa's reindeer draw his sleigh through foggy skies.

Rudolph the Red-Nosed Reindeer

by Johnny Marks

You know Dasher and Dancer and Prancer and Vixen,
Comet and Cupid, and Donder and Blitzen,
But do you recall
The most famous reindeer of all?

Rudolph, the red-nosed reindeer
Had a very shiny nose,
And if you ever saw it,
You would even say it glows.
All of the other reindeer
Used to laugh and call him names,
They never let poor Rudolph
Join in any reindeer games.

Then one foggy Christmas Eve,
Santa came to say,
"Rudolph, with your nose so bright,
Won't you guide my sleigh tonight?"

Then how the reindeer loved him
As they shouted out with glee,
"Rudolph, the red-nosed reindeer,
You'll go down in his-to-ry!"

The Ghost of Christmas Yet to Come

by John R. Bartlit

"Rudolph the Red-Nosed Reindeer," like "The Night Before Christmas," has inspired a number of sequels and parodies. This sad account of Rudolph's efforts to find his way through polluted skies appeared in the *Los Alamos Monitor* for December 17, 1978. Dr. Bartlit, who has a Ph.D. in chemical engineering, works at the Los Alamos National Laboratory. In 1969 his wife and others founded New Mexico Citizens for Clean Air and Water, of which he is now state chairman. His poem was written mainly to arouse the public to visibility degradation caused by air pollution from coal burning at the Four Corners Power Plant in northwestern New Mexico. The poem has been reprinted on many later Christmas occasions. Thanks to the efforts of Bartlit's group, all the power plants in New Mexico have now installed sulfur scrubbers, greatly reducing their damage to the atmosphere.

'Twas the night before Christmas
And all through the skies,
Rudolph was searching
And straining his eyes
By the glow of his nose-light
To see through the smog.
Said Rudolph, "I'm blind
As a flea on a dog!

"I used to enjoy
Flying over these Rockies,
O'er the moonlight on snow—
With the stars as my jockies.
But now I'm bombarded
With ashes and soot,

And I'd make better time
Finding houses on foot."

But he knew that the children
All snug in their beds
Had visions of sugarplums
Still in their heads.
So he bucked up his courage,
And onward he flew—
With a sleigh full of toys
And St. Nicholas, too.

As they finished in Billings,
And started for Butte,
The air became thicker
Where smelters pollute.

They proceeded on course
From Cody to Casper,
But the air was still foul
And Rudolph a gasper.
"We've got to make Denver
By midnight," said Nick.
But both of them felt
Just a little heartsick.

Up there in the air
With just a two-mile vision,
They circled, then made
Quite a tragic decision.
They headed for Boise,
So on through the night—

Each time turning wrong
On their Christmas Eve flight.

Might it be in Los Alamos
On some future year,
That good hilltop children
Will have little to cheer?
On grey Christmas morning,
Poked there in a sock—
They find one skinny present
Instead of a flock.

'Tis a membership gift
At the Clean Air group rate . . .
But by then it will be
Too little . . . too late.

Three Days Before Christmas

by John Langdon

John Langdon is a free-lance artist, writer, and advertising designer who specializes in logos, typographic design, and hand lettering. Since 1988 he has also taught design courses at Drexel University, in Philadelphia. His amusing parody appeared on his 1990 holiday greeting card. I place it in this section because it tells how Rudolph once more came to Santa's rescue.

'Twas three days before Christmas and at the North Pole
not a sound could be heard. Nat even King Cole.[1]

Not a single child's letter had arrived on the scene,
nor a message been left on the answering machine.

Santa's lap had been largely ignored at the mall;
on the 800 line there had not been one call.

Not a workshop was busy, not a toy being made;
even the reindeer were somewhat dismayed.

"It's this darned recession," Santa had grumbled.
"Seems like a depression," the missus had mumbled.

The elves were all sleeping in little elf beds
while nightmares of overtime danced in their heads.

Their tools and their aprons were laid out with care
in hopes that some work orders soon would be there.

Mrs. Claus and her husband (still wearing his cap)
had just settled down and were trying to nap.

"Things are usually busy at this time of year,"
Santa thought to himself as he brushed back a tear.

1. A reference to the singer Nat "King" Cole.

When all of a sudden there arose such a ringing
he sprang from his bed to see what was dinging.

Then laying a finger alongside his nose
up to his second floor office he rose.

The moon gave a lustre to the snow in the night
but once in the office he needed more light.

He flipped on the switch and he looked all around
but nothing appeared to have just made a sound.

He'd hoped 'twas a phone call. It very well could be,
but no phones were ringing or looked like they should be.

"Perhaps I just dreamed it," he said to himself.
"I'm getting to be such a foolish old elf."

"But still," he muttered, "I just have a hunch . . ."
and right at that moment he heard a small crunch.

His head spun around, his eyes sharp as tacks,
as a sliver of paper emerged from the fax.

The crunching continued, the paper grew longer . . .
a cover sheet made his curiosity grow stronger.

As page two began his eyes started to mist.
Could it be? Yes it was! A child's Christmas list!

He raced from the office and made such a clatter
Mrs. Claus came running to see what was the matter.

"I've got work! A client! An order to fill!"
By now his voice had gotten quite shrill.

"Settle down, Santa," Mrs. Claus hissed.
"You'll wake up the elves, and there's *only* one list.

"You've had rush jobs before and you've always come
    through.
You're acting like this was all something quite new."

He was just calming down and began to relax
when another ring came from the telephone/fax.

Then what to their wondering eyes should appear
but a second child's Christmas-wish-list of the year.

Then a third, and a fourth, and soon they lost count
as the pile of curled fax paper started to mount.

The elves were assembled and they anxiously listened
to Santa's announcement. Each little eye glistened.

"That fax machine purchase has finally paid off!
It's Christmas again! Not one elf will be laid off!"

As dry leaves before the wild hurricane fly,
the elves flew to their work, the lists stacked to the sky.

The reindeer, who'd begun to doubt their existence
now were required to lend their assistance.

"On Dasher, on Dancer, on Comet and Cupid!
We'll fulfill every wish, no matter how stupid!

"On Prancer and Vixen, on Blitzen and Donder!"
It was then that Santa's mind started to wander.

He'd thought of a thought that caused him to shiver.
"Oh, how," he wondered, "will I ever deliver?

"If we get these toys finished in time—and we *might*,
neither I nor my reindeer'll be fit for a flight."

'Twas then that one reindeer I know you'll recall
(he *was* the most famous reindeer of them all)

Came in to the workshop to make a suggestion:
"I have an idea I can answer your question."

"Why, Rudolph, my deer," Santa greeted him sadly.
I need a solution to this problem badly."

"How will I ever get out of this mess?"
Answered Rudolph quite simply, "Call Federal Express."

Richard Steele, in a letter to the *Chicago Tribune* (December 21, 1990) made the tongue-in-cheek suggestion that May got the idea for Rudolph's red nose from the rosy, pimply nose of Corporal Bardolph in the first part of Shakespeare's *King Henry IV*, Act 3, Scene 3. Sir John Falstaff, drinking in the Boar's Head Tavern with Bardolph, likens his friend's nose, red from boozing, to "an ignis fatuus or a ball of fire" and to an "everlasting bonfire light." He calls Bardolph "the Knight of the Burning Lamp." The glowing nose, says Falstaff, has saved him a thousand marks in torches by lighting up the road at night when the two wander from tavern to tavern. "What's next?" Steele concluded his letter. "The rotund Falstaff himself as a model for Santa?"

"Christmas
for
Ever!"

EPILOGUE: A SHOP OF GHOSTS

by G. K. Chesterton

Gilbert Keith Chesterton (1874–1936), who loved the Yuletide season as much as Charles Dickens did, often wrote about it. This tribute to England's Father Christmas is from G.K.'s 1909 collection of essays, *Tremendous Trifles*. It had earlier appeared in London's *Daily News*, which explains why Chesterton says you can obtain it for a halfpenny. I cannot imagine a more appropriate ending for this anthology.

Nearly all the best and most precious things in the universe you can get for a halfpenny. I make an exception, of course, of the sun, the moon, the earth, people, stars, thunderstorms, and such trifles. You can get them for nothing. Also I make an exception of another thing, which I am not allowed to mention in this paper, and of which the lowest price is a penny halfpenny. But the general principle will be at once apparent. In the street behind me, for instance, you can now get a ride on an electric tram for a halfpenny. To be on an electric tram is to be on a flying castle in a fairy tale. You can get quite a large number of brightly coloured sweets for a halfpenny. Also you can get the chance of reading this article for a halfpenny; along, of course, with other and irrelevant matter.

But if you want to see what a vast and bewildering array of valuable things you can get at a halfpenny each you should do as I was doing last night. I was gluing my nose against the glass of a very small and dimly lit toy shop in one of the greyest and leanest of the streets of Battersea. But dim as was that square of light, it was filled (as a child once said to me) with all the colours God ever made. Those toys of the poor were like the children who buy them; they were all dirty; but they were all bright. For my part, I think brightness more important than cleanliness; since the first is of the soul, and the second of the body. You must excuse me; I am a democrat; I know I am out of fashion in the modern world.

As I looked at that palace of pigmy wonders, at small green omnibuses, at small blue elephants, at small black dolls, and small red Noah's arks, I must have fallen into some sort of unnatural trance. That lit shop-window became like the brilliantly lit stage when one is watching some highly coloured comedy. I forgot the grey houses and the grimy people behind me as one forgets the dark galleries and the dim crowds at a theatre. It seemed as if the little objects behind the glass were small, not because they were toys, but because they were objects far away. The green omnibus was really a green omnibus, a green Bayswater omnibus, passing across some huge desert on its ordinary way to Bayswater. The blue elephant was no longer blue with paint; he was blue with distance. The black doll was really a negro relieved against passionate tropic foliage in the land where every weed is flaming and only man is black. The red Noah's ark was really the enormous ship of earthly salvation riding on the rain-swollen sea, red in the first morning of hope.

Every one, I suppose, knows such stunning instants of abstraction, such brilliant blanks in the mind. In such moments one can see the face of one's own best friend as an unmeaning pattern of spectacles or moustaches. They are commonly marked by the two signs of the slowness of their growth and the suddenness of their termination. The return to real thinking is often as abrupt as bumping into a man. Very often indeed (in my case) it *is* bumping into a man. But in any case the awakening is always emphatic and, generally speaking, it is always complete. Now, in this case, I did come back with a shock of sanity to the consciousness that I was, after all, only staring into a dingy little toy-shop; but in some strange way the mental cure did not seem to be final. There was still in my mind an unmanageable something that told me that I had strayed into some odd atmosphere, or that I had already done some odd thing. I felt as if I had worked a miracle or committed a sin. It was as if I had at any rate, stepped across some border in the soul.

To shake off this dangerous and dreamy sense I went into the shop and tried to buy wooden soldiers. The man in the shop was very old and broken, with confused white hair covering his head and half his face, hair so startlingly white that it looked almost artificial. Yet though he was senile and even sick, there was nothing of suffering in his eyes; he looked rather as if he were gradually falling asleep in a not unkindly decay. He gave me the wooden soldiers, but when I put down the money he did not at first seem to see it; then he blinked at it feebly, and then he pushed it feebly away.

"No, no," he said vaguely. "I never have. I never have. We are rather old-fashioned here."

"Not taking money," I replied, "seems to me more like an uncommonly new fashion than an old one."

"I never have," said the old man, blinking and blowing his nose; "I've always given presents. I'm too old to stop."

"Good heavens!" I said. "What can you mean? Why, you might be Father Christmas."

"I am Father Christmas," he said apologetically, and blew his nose again.

The lamps could not have been lighted yet in the street outside. At any rate, I could see nothing against the darkness but the shining shop-window. There were no sounds of steps or voices in the street; I might have strayed into some new and sunless world. But something had cut the chords of

common sense, and I could not feel even surprise except sleepily. Something made me say, "You look ill, Father Christmas."

"I am dying," he said.

I did not speak, and it was he who spoke again.

"All the new people have left my shop. I cannot understand it. They seem to object to me on such curious and inconsistent sort of grounds, these scientific men, and these innovators. They say that I give people superstitions and make them too visionary; they say I give people sausages and make them too coarse. They say my heavenly parts are too heavenly; they say my earthly parts are too earthly; I don't know what they want, I'm sure. How can heavenly things be too heavenly, or earthly things too earthly? How can one be too good, or too jolly? I don't understand. But I understand one thing well enough. These modern people are living and I am dead."

"You may be dead," I replied. "You ought to know. But as for what they are doing—do not call it living."

A silence fell suddenly between us which I somehow expected to be unbroken. But it had not fallen for more than a few seconds when, in the utter stillness, I distinctly heard a very rapid step coming nearer and nearer along the street. The next moment a figure flung itself into the shop and stood framed in the doorway. He wore a large white hat tilted back as if in impatience; he had tight black old-fashioned pantaloons, a gaudy old-fashioned stock and waistcoat, and an old fantastic coat. He had large, wide-open, luminous eyes like those of an arresting actor; he had a pale, nervous face, and a fringe of beard. He took in the shop and the old man in a look that seemed literally a flash and uttered the exclamation of a man utterly staggered.

"Good lord!" he cried out; "it can't be you! It isn't you! I came to ask where your grave was."

"I'm not dead yet, Mr. Dickens," said the old gentleman, with a feeble smile; "but I'm dying," he hastened to add reassuringly.

"But, dash it all, you were dying in my time," said Mr.

Charles Dickens with animation; "and you don't look a day older."

"I've felt like this for a long time," said Father Christmas.

Mr. Dickens turned his back and put his head out of the door into the darkness.

"Dick," he roared at the top of his voice; "he's still alive."

Another shadow darkened the doorway, and a much larger and more full-blooded gentleman in an enormous periwig came in, fanning his flushed face with a military hat of the cut of Queen Anne. He carried his head well back like a soldier, and his hot face had even a look of arrogance, which was suddenly contradicted by his eyes, which were literally as humble as a dog's. His sword made a great clatter, as if the shop were too small for it.

"Indeed," said Sir Richard Steele, " 'tis a most prodigious matter, for the man was dying when I wrote about Sir Roger de Coverley and his Christmas Day."

My senses were growing dimmer and the room darker. It seemed to be filled with newcomers.

"It hath ever been understood," said a burly man, who carried his head humorously and obstinately a little on one side—I think he was Ben Jonson—"It hath ever been understood, consule Jacobo, under our King James and her late Majesty, that such good and hearty customs were fallen sick, and like to pass from the world. This grey beard most surely was no lustier when I knew him than now."

And I also thought I heard a green-clad man, like Robin Hood, say in some mixed Norman French, "But I saw the man dying."

"I have felt like this a long time," said Father Christmas, in his feeble way again.

Mr. Charles Dickens suddenly leant across to him.

"Since when?" he asked. "Since you were born?"

"Yes," said the old man, and sank shaking into a chair. "I have been always dying."

Mr. Dickens took off his hat with a flourish like a man calling a mob to rise.

"I understand it now," he cried, "you will never die."

Permissions

Every effort has been made to trace the ownership of copyrighted material and to obtain permission from copyright holders. If any question arises about the use of any material, we will make the necessary corrections in future printings. Thanks are due to the following authors, publishers, publications, and agents for permission to use the material indicated.

Armand Ringer, for "Santa Changes His Mind."
James Van Alen, for "After Santa Had Departed."
Rolaine Hochstein, and Curtis Brown, Ltd., for "Going My Way?"
Mary Ann Madden and *New York* magazine, for the prize-winning parodies of the magazine's 1973 competition.
Frank Jacobs and *Mad* magazine, for parodies that appeared in *Mad*.
Hugh Mulligan, for "A Visit from Jack Nicklaus."
John Doyel, for "A Farm Visit from St. Hick."
Kay Dee, for "Christmas in Cygnus."
Gerald Weales, for "The Night Before the Morning After."
Donald Morris, for "Rush to Passage."
Charlotte Van Bebber Cohen, for " 'Twas the Night Before Christmas in the Desert."

Dave Morice, for "A Visit from St. Numismatist" and "A Visit from St. Alphabet."

Kathleen Kustin, for "The Night Before the Topology Final."

David Bradley, Betty Cheng, Dan LaLiberte, Hal Render, and Grego Roberts, for "The Worm Before Christmas."

William Dunning, for "Holmes and Watson Have a Visitor."

The Kimberly-Clark Corporation, for "A Visit from St. Quickolas."

Eliot Pfanstiehl, for "The Night Before Thanksgiving."

Peter Eichenstaedt, for "Adobe Joe's Christmas."

Lalo Guerrero, for "Pancho Claus."

Kenin Scannell, for "De Night Before de Christmas."

Sandra Rokoff, for "Get With It, Santa Baby."

James Rice and Pelican Publishing Company, for Rice's "Texas Night Before Christmas" and "Prairie Night Before Christmas."

Pelican Publishing Company, for J. B. Kling's "Cajun Night Before Christmas" and Thomas Turner's "Hillbilly Night Afore Christmas."

The National Education Association," for "An Educator's Night Before Christmas," by Jean Horneck and Dorothy Waleski.

Michael Marks, for the lyrics of "Rudolph the Red-Nosed Reindeer."

John Bartlit, for "The Ghost of Christmas Yet to Come."

ABOUT THE AUTHOR

Martin Gardner is best known as a science writer who for twenty-five years wrote *Scientific American*'s "Mathematical Games" column. These columns have been appearing in book form, of which there are now thirteen volumes. He has also written a theological novel, *The Flight of Peter Fromm*; many books about physics, philosophy, and pseudoscience; numerous juveniles; technical books on conjuring; and several collections of essays and book reviews. His literary criticism includes *The Annotated Alice*, *The Annotated Ancient Mariner*, *The Annotated Snark*, *The Annotated Casey at the Bat*, and a recently published *More Annotated Alice*.

Born in 1914, in Tulsa, Gardner was a newspaper reporter in Tulsa and a public relations writer at his alma mater, the University of Chicago, before his four-year stint in the Navy during World War II. Bucknell has given him an honorary doctorate, and he has received several awards for his writings about mathematics and science. *The Whys of a Philosophical Scrivener* is his "confessional," defending what he calls his "philosophical theism." He and his wife, Charlotte, live in the mountains of western North Carolina.